SECRET CHICHESTER

Philip MacDougall

AMBERLEY

To Charlotte, David and Vikki.

First published 2016

Amberley Publishing
The Hill, Stroud
Gloucestershire, GL5 4EP

www.amberley-books.com

Copyright © Philip MacDougall, 2016

The right of Philip MacDougall to be identified as the
Author of this work has been asserted in accordance
with the Copyrights, Designs and Patents Act 1988.

ISBN 978 1 4456 5039 5 (print)
ISBN 978 1 4456 5040 1 (ebook)

British Library Cataloguing in Publication Data.
A catalogue record for this book is available from the
British Library.

Typesetting by Amberley Publishing.
Printed in Great Britain.

Contents

Preface

In this account of the ancient city of Chichester I have chosen to look at aspects of history rather than providing a more general survey. The latter is easily found elsewhere, thus allowing this book to take a glimpse at areas of Chichester's past that are less commonly known. In this respect I am using the word 'secret' in a less literal sense, something that is generally not so well known.

In researching this book I have drawn heavily on primary sources, including newspapers and original documents. A list of these will be found in the bibliography at the end of this book.

1. The Little and Lost Churches

Strange as it might seem, within the walls of the old city there were once eight medieval churches, each with its own parish. This is quite staggering given that the walls enclose only an area of about 100 acres and the total population of the city during the Middle Ages was likely to have been somewhere in the region of 1,000. In searching out these churches, it provides a nice little excuse for a leisurely walk around the historic city. For this reason, it is not my intention to take a chronological approach to this particular secret history of Chichester – for many of these churches are either well-hidden or long-since demolished – but an approach more easily followed by the casual peramble.

A good starting point is the corner of Guildhall Street and Priory Lane, close to the entrance to Priory Park. Here, on a site that is now part of the Ship Hotel, stood the first of these parish churches, St Peter *sub castro* (Latin for St John-under-the-Castle). Serving only this immediate corner of the city, this was a small oblong post-conquest church that was to be completely demolished in 1574. Long before that date however, it had ceased being a parish church, having been given over to the Hospital of St Mary's, a medieval foundation serving the needs of the sick, the poor, and travellers. Before leaving the Priory Park area it's worth taking a look inside the park. Formerly the site of a medieval

Detail of the area around Priory Park from a map of the city as surveyed by George Loader in 1812. Clearly marked and within the area of Priory Park is the Town Hall (more usually referred to today as the old Guildhall or Priory); also discernible (with difficulty) is St Peter's church. The road, now known as St Peter's, did not exist in 1812.

monastery, the Guildhall (which stands in the centre of the Park) was once the monastery chapel. Within the park is also a raised earthen area, this originally a mound or motte that would have been built by Earl Roger de Montgomery, the first ruler of the city under the Normans, and upon which would have been constructed a wooden castle or keep and from where the church of St Peter gained its designation, *sub castro*.

Keeping Priory Park to the left, a short walk along Priory Road will bring us to the Park Tavern and a road on the right simply named St Peter's. At the far end of this street, where it feeds into North Street (but with the road sign now declaring it to be St Peter's), once stood St Peter the Less, the largest of the city's medieval churches. Originally constructed in the thirteenth century, it began life with only a nave and chancel but during the following century it gained a south aisle and tower. Demolished in 1957, the space that it once occupied has now given way to both the road that now bears its name and a large shop (currently Lakeland) that stands on the south side of St Peter's with the front of this same shop on North Street.

The building in the foreground and glimpsed through the open gate of Priory Park stands on the site once occupied by the medieval parish church of St Peter *sub castro*.

St Peters, once the largest of the city's medieval churches, was demolished in 1957 to make way for a shop and a roadway that now commemorates the church through use of the name St Peter.

At this point it is probably best to return along St Peter's (or St Peters) before turning sharp right into St Martin's Square. At the far end of St Martin's Square, past the medieval St Mary's cottages and following the road as it dog-legs, a small gated garden will be reached. The garden is opened only on week days, with the high ancient walls that surround it once belonging to Chichester's third parish church, that of St Martin's or, somewhat less elegantly, St Martin's in the Pig Market. Once composed of a nave, chancel and bell tower, much of the building was demolished in 1906. At the time of its demolition, a thirteenth-century wall painting was uncovered, this depicting a bishop with mitre and crozier and assumed by many to be an image of St Richard (the patron saint of Sussex).

With or without an apostrophe? The street which celebrates the former medieval parish church of St Peter's is confusingly apostrophised at one end but not the other!

On the northeast corner of St Martin's Street here viewed through its open gateway, is one of Chichester's secret little gardens, this formed out of the ancient walls of the former thirteenth-century parish church of St Martin's.

Open most weekdays, the garden surrounded by the ancient walls of St Martin's provides a restful respite from the daily grind.

On leaving the garden, turn right and then immediately left into Lion Street. Mid-way along Lion Street note the small marker stone, engraved with S. O. and the year 1706, which formerly marked the north-east boundary of a further medieval parish, that of St Olave's . The actual church of St Olave's (now a redundant church) stands on the east side of North Street and is reached (after a short walk) by taking a left-hand turn at the end of Lion Street. Now a Christian bookshop, it is to be easily found by way of the large blue board mounted on the wall of this ancient building and which announces the former parish church to be of Saxon origin.

Despite this claim of St Olave's being Saxon in origin, this is a fact difficult to confirm. The church saw much rebuilding during the Middle Ages with heavy restoration work carried out in the nineteenth century. The only visible evidence of a possible Saxon date is the inner south doorway, being tall, narrow and shaped in the Saxon style. Any real evidence of such an early date, it is supposed, must lie in the undercroft located below the floor of the chancel. Now blocked and inaccessible, those who carried out restoration work in 1851 came across many reused Roman tiles, a practice common in Saxon times. Also to be noted in St Olave's is a carefully worked fourteenth-century piscine.

On leaving St Olave's and continuing along North Street, the sixteenth-century market cross should not be ignored, this given to the city by Bishop Story in 1501. The area behind the buildings lying within the angle formed by the junction of South and East streets was where the church of St Peter in the Market once stood, this serving, by 1229, a parish of two inhabitants. In that year Ralph, Bishop of Chichester, petitioned Henry III to demolish the church. While this request was apparently granted, there is evidence that the building survived a further two centuries, serving as a chapel to St Mary's Hospital (the same medieval foundation that had previously acquired St Peter *sub castro*).

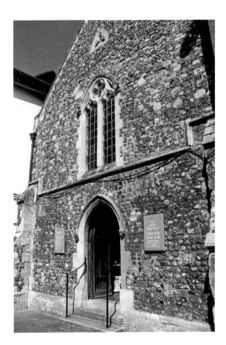

Generally considered to be the earliest of Chichester's medieval churches is that of St Olave's – this being of possible Saxon origin.

Close to St Martin's is the medieval charity 'The Hospital of the Blessed Mary', commonly called St Mary's Hospital. Upon being deemed no longer parish churches, both St Peter *sub castro* and St Peter in the Market, were given over to this charity to help in its work of supporting Chichester's poor and sick.

The early thirteenth-century church of All Saints in West Pallant, now the offices of an investment management company.

The now blocked former south entrance to All Saints church.

Passing round the cross, a short walk along South Street will bring us to West Pallant on the left and where the sixth of the ancient parish churches, All Saints, is to be found. Relatively little altered, having survived into the twenty-first century, it is early thirteenth century in origin. The outer walls are of flint with stone dressing while the north wall is covered with rough cast that has now been partly chipped away to reveal some original features. A simple un-aisled building with small lancet windows cut into the north and south walls, it has a renewed triplet window to the east. A seventh medieval parish church also once stood in the Pallants, this on the corner of Baffin's Lane and taking the name of St Andrew's in the Pallant. Little is known of this church, other than it being mentioned in 1199 and 1289, probably ceasing to exist soon after that date. That the Pallant area of Chichester should have two separate parish churches during the Middle Ages possibly relates to it having been an area once administered separately from the rest of the city due to it being under the jurisdiction of the Archbishop of Canterbury.

The church of St John the Evangelist in St John's Street is unmistakably Georgian, built of white brick in the neo-classical tradition. Dating to 1812, it was constructed at a cost of £7,000. Although never serving a medieval parish, the church itself is well worth viewing.

St Andrew Oxmarket situated on the north side of East Street was built during the thirteenth century and refitted early in the nineteenth century.

An early sixteenth-century memorial tablet on the west wall of St Andrew Oxmarket; although much decayed, the kneeling figures of a man, his wife, and sons and daughters are just discernible.

Returning to the market cross and entering East Street the last of the city's eight medieval parish churches, St Andrew Oxmarket, can be approached either by way St Martin's Street or a narrow passage leading directly off East Street and marked by a finger post that points towards the Chichester Centre of Art and which, in fact, is the church. St Andrew's is another of the surviving churches of the city and continues to serve the community as the art gallery to which the finger post points. Of stone and flint construction, the church is another small and simple rectangular building that appears to date to the late thirteenth century. The north and south walls are pierced by windows of several styles, these representing differing phases in the advance of medieval architecture, while the east lancet is a modern addition. Entry into the church is well-rewarded, not only because of the art work frequently on display, but because of a number of interesting monuments to be found on the walls of the building.

In returning to the market cross and entering West Street a ninth medieval parish and the largest in the city has now been reached, the subdeanery and which until the nineteenth century did not have its own parish church. Instead, those living in the parish were served by an altar located in the north transept of the cathedral. This was a less than satisfactory arrangement as only one service was allowed per week, this on Sundays and latterly in the afternoon, while the space provided by the transept was of an inadequate size for the assembled congregation. As the population of this parish continued to grow in size, it was decided, during the nineteenth century, to build a separate church and name it St Peter the Great, otherwise the church of the subdeanery. The idea for this church was certainly under discussion in 1847 when the dean and chapter of the cathedral launched an appeal to raise money, a site on the corner of West Street and Tower Street having already been found. The first stone of the new church was laid in August 1848 with the building completed in mid-1852. As originally planned, the church was to have had a west tower but this was never constructed due to escalating costs. Nowadays, this former church building is better known as West's bar and lounge.

Outside of the city wall, it might be noted, is to be found one further medieval church and two churches that replaced those destroyed during a siege of the city undertaken by Parliamentary troops during the Civil War. These are best visited separately as no easy walk can be designed that will encompass all of them in a reasonable amount of walking time.

One medieval parish did not have a separate church, parishioners living on the west side of the city served by only an altar in the north transept of the cathedral. This print shows damage to the transept following the collapse of the central tower and spire in February 1861. By that date, however, a parish church had been built to serve the parish of St Peter the Great.

A modern-day view of the north transept and a glimpse of the tower that had to be completely rebuilt following the earlier collapse.

St Peter the Great was built in the mid-nineteenth century and is now better known to most Cicestrians as West's Bar.

A more general view of St Peter the Great in West Street. Although relatively short-lived as a church, the surviving birth, marriage and burial registers for this parish go back to the sixteenth century. This is because the church took over the earlier parish of the subdeanery that had been served by the altar located in the cathedral.

Detail of the former parish church of St Peter the Great shows that it was carefully modelled upon the medieval Gothic-style of the fourteenth century.

St Bartholomew's in Mount Lane. Totally destroyed in 1642, it was completely rebuilt and consecrated by the Bishop of Chichester on 20 July 1832. As for the original church, this was circular (rather than cruciform) in design, being an attempt to replicate the Holy Sepulchre in Jerusalem.

A view of the interior of St Bartholomew's as it appeared in or around the 1930s. No longer a parish church, it is now part of University of Chichester and is in use as a classroom and chaplaincy centre.

Evidence of an earlier church on the St Bartholomew's site is clear from the gravestones in the former church yard, many of these dating to the early eighteenth century.

The church of medieval construction is the now redundant St Mary's (Whyke Road) and which dates to the eleventh century but with thirteenth-century additions and a north aisle dating to 1866. It has since been converted into offices. Of the two churches rebuilt following their destruction in the Civil War, these are St Pancras (just beyond East Gate at the beginning of the road known as St Pancras) and St Bartholomew (Mount Lane). St Pancras, which was originally constructed sometime around the thirteenth century, was rebuilt in the mid-eighteenth century with a north aisle added in 1869. St Bartholomew's was more certainly of the thirteenth century and rebuilt in the renaissance style in 1832.

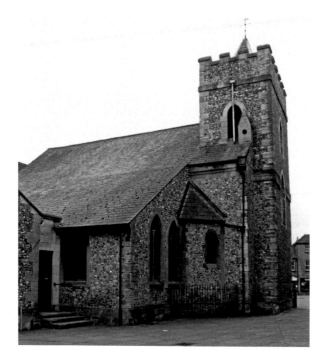

St Pancras in West Gate. Although having a medieval appearance, this church was actually built between 1850 and 1851, albeit on the site of an earlier church.

The now redundant church of St Mary's (Whyke Road) which dates to the eleventh century.

St Paul's church, consecrated by the Bishop of Chichester in October 1836, was built to meet the needs of a rapidly expanding population that was then being housed in the Broyle.

St George's was another Anglican church built to meet the needs of a rapidly growing population outside the immediate city. The foundation stone of the church was laid by the Mayor of Chichester in September 1901. On hand to mark the occasion was a military band.

All Saints, Portfield, was completed in 1871. The parish it served had formerly been part of the parish of Oving. That it made sense for a new church to be built resulted from the expansion of the Portfield area of Chichester and that of Oving church being more than two miles from Portfield. To provide the church with a medieval feel, its walls of concrete were given a flint facing on the outside. Declared redundant in 1981, the building for a time housed a doll and mechanical musical instrument museum.

DID YOU KNOW?

Early evidence of religious worship in Chichester comes in the form of the so-called Jupiter stone, discovered in 1934 during an archaeological excavation in West Street. Dating to the Roman period and now on display in the museum, it is thought to have formed part of the base that would have been surmounted by a statue to Jupiter, the king of all gods.

The churches of St Paul (Broyle Road), All Saints, Portfield (Church Road) and St George (Cleveland Road) although built in the thirteenth-century style are much more modern, St Paul's completed in 1836, All Saints in 1871 and St George's in 1902.

Within a cavity of the foundation stone of the church of St Peter the Great in West Street, laid in August 1848, is a bottle containing coins of the period beneath a plate cast in the form of a Maltese Cross that had been discovered in the cemetery of the cathedral.

2. The Swell Mob

And the reason we're all here:
the 2011 Glorious Goodwood.

For Cicestrians, Goodwood is a second home, a summer playground with one of the most famous racecourses in the country. But Cicestrians are not the only ones drawn to Goodwood on race days, for they share such occasions with thousands of others from London and throughout Great Britain. 'Glorious Goodwood', in particular, brings bustling crowds both on to the Downs and into the heart of Chichester, providing local businesses, especially restaurateurs, with an influx of free spenders. However, be warned. Where such crowds gather, there are those who are looking to take advantage.

Forget 'Honest Joe' the bookmaker, for while the odds are stacked in Joe's favour, there's always the slight chance of a return on a carefully made investment. No, it's not him that needs to be avoided but the professional criminal. Doubtless some are still to be found at the racecourse during Goodwood week, but in earlier decades the family men and the flash mob posed serious problems that led to a great deal of misery. Composed of vicious criminals down from 'the smoke', these gang members were regular attenders at Glorious Goodwood, using various ploys and scams to fleece the unwary.

For maintaining law and order on race days, the county police formed in 1857, with headquarters in Chichester's Southgate, eventually took responsibility. Before arrival on the scene of the county police, racing at Goodwood having been introduced by the 3rd Duke of Richmond (1750–1806) with the course constructed in 1802, much reliance had been placed on the presence of soldiers from either the barracks in Chichester or the Sussex Militia and of which the 5th Duke of Richmond (1819–1860) was their long-time colonel. Adorned in bright red jackets and white trousers, regimental soldiers and militia men provided a highly visible threat to any small-time criminal, easily quelling the ambitions of lawbreakers before things got serious. Of course, the various

GOING TO THE RACES.—HIGH-STREET, CHICHESTER.

It's August 1846 and the streets of Chichester are crowded with race-goers on their way to the Downs on Cup Day.

'Honest Joe' loses again. It's not a total rarity to come away from Glorious Goodwood with more than you brought to the races.

A view of the Grandstand at Goodwood as seen in 1862. Only those of high social standing could gain access to the Grandstand with its saloon, banqueting hall and terrace. Beyond, and somewhat exaggerated in height, lies the Trundle.

The crowded racecourse for another Glorious Goodwood – but the style of dress is very different.

holders of the Richmond title, in being so well connected and having a lock-up sited close to the racecourse could easily ensure that those arrested were quickly convicted. But with the summer races becoming increasingly popular the attendance of those with criminal intent not only increased, but organised gangs began finding their way to Goodwood. While the family men were a loose collection of thieves, pickpockets and gamblers, the swell mob was much more organised. Looking out for each other, members of the mob rarely worked alone. A favoured trick was for one of the swell's 'buzz-men' to approach an elderly woman and attempt to 'buzz' or converse with her. The buzz-man's intention was to frighten the woman by a few uncalled-for comments. Shortly afterwards his 'pol' or young female companion would offer to assist the victim by consoling her but, in so doing, would use her nimble fingers to remove a purse or some valuable item of jewellery.

Members of the swell mob were smart, not just in their approach to crime but also in appearance. Dressed in the height of fashion at the time, the young gentlemen of the mob would puff cigars and fondle the finest mosaic jewellery. It was not easy to distinguish them from the equally fashionable genteel folk who expected to gain exclusive entry, by ticket of

Looking towards the finishing line and in the general direction of the Trundle.

An early twentieth-century photograph of the Goodwood stand that had originally been built in 1830 and was shortly to be replaced.

course, into the specially built grandstand that was reserved for those of a certain bourgeois or aristocratic standing. To keep the swell buzz-men and their pols out, members of the Sussex militia proved to be not a jot of use, unable to distinguish a swell from ordinary folk. Instead, the duke turned to the Bow Street Runners. Originally founded in 1742 and overseen by the Bow Street magistrates' office, they were funded by central government and could put in an appearance anywhere in the country where serious crime was a problem. Of even greater value was that Bow Street Runners were more than just a little familiar with the swell mob, usually in a position to put a name to a face. Standing guard by each entrance to the grandstand that had been first erected in 1801 and replaced by a larger one in 1830, a couple of Bow Street Runners would simply collar the swells and, with the help of a few soldiers, either arrest them or turn them away. Among those especially sought was Harry 'The Elephant' Prendergast, one of the leaders of the mob. Of stout appearance but always respectably dressed, he frequently put in an appearance at Goodwood, accompanied by an elderly pol who gave the impression of being his nurse rather than a dexterous fingersmith.

Looking towards the March Stand – the premium hospitality option for enthusiasts who wish to combine luxury and race-going.

Following the formation of the Metropolitan Police in 1829, the Bow Street Runners were replaced at Goodwood by a sergeant and number of constables from Westminster's A Division. With such precautions being taken, Goodwood just about clung on to its reputation of exclusivity, something that it came close to losing in 1849 when a member of the London swell mob brazenly walked up to Lord John Scott, the 2nd Earl of Eldon, an enthusiastic race-goer, and snatched from him a gold watch and chain. It was a deed carried out in full view of numerous spectators. Several soldiers attempted to retrieve the watch but were, themselves, set upon by about twenty or thirty of the swell mob. The London flash successfully rescued their fellow swell, securing also the gold watch that he had stolen. Although no mention is made of the Metropolitan Police being present that year or of any of the swell mob being arrested, several lesser criminals were brought before the county bench in Chichester. They included two thieves, one a female who had stolen a handkerchief and the other for stealing a gold watch, but not the one taken from Lord John Scott. Also brought before the bench at Chichester on that occasion was a gamer charged with playing the pea and a thimble trick (a sleight-of-hand swindling game).

Given that there was no repetition in future years at Goodwood of such open attacks on high-profile members of the aristocracy as had been inflicted on Lord John Scott, it seems that A Division may well have been suitably reinforced with a larger number of constables. Either way, confidence in Goodwood as somewhere that was safe for the well-heeled was quickly restored, a point confirmed by the mass circulation *Penny Illustrated Paper* which informed its readers in 1862,

Without parading rules more suited to an assembly of Covenanters than a company met together for the purpose of amusement, good precautions are put together to avoid licence to stray into licentiousness. In all that has relation to the convenience and enjoyment of its visitors there is nothing left uncared for. The grand stand with its saloons, banquet halls, terraces and parterres lying in a pleasant shade is a fitting place where the noble and gentle may meet and mingle, while for the humbler holiday folk there is a splendid course for promenade during the interval between the races.

Two years later the *Penny Illustrated Paper* felt sufficiently confident in favourably contrasting Goodwood with Epsom, a racecourse that many of the gentry were now avoiding,

> At Epsom every rank, from the very highest to the lowest, is blended in indiscernible gradations, and the crowd which assembles on the Downs is, for the time being, only a houseless London, carrying with it all the extravagance and squalor, all the vice, folly and enjoyment, of the great metropolis itself.

While at Goodwood,

> The line is broad and well defined which separates high and low.

One other swell mob success did however, take place in 1865 when members of the mob carried out a well-planned attack on the Careless refreshment booth. This was on the last evening of Goodwood week, the swells aware that shortly before 6 p.m. A Division usually returned to London, leaving only a small body of the West Sussex Constabulary. Waiting for that moment, the mob created a disturbance in the betting enclosure at the side of the refreshment booth. With all eyes turned on what was happening here, other members of the swell mob cut through the side of the booth and grabbed the cash box that contained the day's takings of £50.

A crime connected with the Goodwood meeting and brought before the county bench in Chichester, and much to the horror of many Cicestrians, was that of animal cruelty. This was in August 1886 and related to the condition of horses being used to convey passengers from Chichester to the racecourse. To meet the huge demand that arose

No. 4 West Street Chichester (to the middle of this photograph). At the beginning of the twentieth century this was a tobacconist shop run be Henry Millington but also operating as an off-course betting shop when such activities were illegal. Raided by the police in August 1914, Henry Millington was fined £50. While this might sound a lot, it needs to be weighed against the fact that Millington was making a clear profit each year that was well in excess of £4,000.

during Goodwood Week, carriages and horses were brought to Chichester from London and it was the poor condition of these horses, underfed and often savagely whipped, that gave rise to some twenty prosecutions that resulted in fines of between £1 and £3. An inspiration behind such prosecutions was Anna Sewell's novel *Black Beauty* and which highlighted the cruelties inflicted upon London cab horses. For a short period of her life Anna Sewell had lived on the outskirts of Chichester at Graylingwell Farm in the Summersdale area.

Not unexpectedly the huge crowds arriving during Goodwood Week and passing through Chichester also brought problems to the city. The dense crowds on the London-bound platform of the station was a further easy target for light-fingered thieves, but not often reported as the victim rarely knew that a pocket had been picked, assuming it to be an unfortunate loss of a wallet or purse. Another illegality that descended on Chichester was that of off-course bookies operating from illegal betting shops. While Chichester, today, has several betting shops, such ventures did not become legal until 1961. One such illegal operation was uncovered during Goodwood Week 1914 when Portsmouth detectives and Chichester-based police descended on Henry Millington's tobacco shop in West Street. Millington, together with several of the assistants he employed in the shop were arrested for receiving ready money for betting and heavily fined. It seems to have been a very profitable business, with Millington apparently having banked over £4,000 since the beginning of the year. In some ways, the police operation had a certain comical element to it, given that the detectives were in disguise for the purpose of collecting evidence. According to a report that later appeared in the *Portsmouth News*, one Portsmouth detective wore an apron while carrying his boots under his arm while another simply had his sleeves rolled up!

A contemporary newspaper illustration of the bare-knuckle prize fight held at Goodwood in 1888.

The arrest of Charley Mitchell.

DID YOU KNOW?

Over time 'Glorious Goodwood' became one of the social events of the year, the last one of the summer before high society adjourned to the Highlands of Scotland for the 'Glorious Twelfth' when grouse shooting begins.

Goodwood was once the venue for bare-knuckle prize fights. Particularly popular among the working class, these fights had few rules, with opponents battering each other through endless rounds, until only one remained standing. One such fight was broken up by the police in August 1888. Among those arrested was Charley Mitchell, undoubtedly the nation's most famous boxer. Although he was known as a bare-knuckle boxer, he mostly fought with gloves under the legal London Prize Ring Rules. His crime on this occasion was not bare-knuckle fighting but being part of the very sizeable crowd that had gathered on the Downs to watch bare-knuckle boxers Camp and Hullett beat each other senseless.

Lord William Lennox, a younger son of the 4th Duke of Richmond almost missed Glorious Goodwood in 1871 due to an argument with a London cabman. The cab had been called to his London residence to take some of his family to Victoria station for a train to Chichester but they failed to pay the final two pence and the cabman took Lord Lennox to court during Goodwood week, forcing him to return to London where he appeared in court and was required to pay the cabman two pence and the additional court costs of three shillings. Lord William is best known as Lord Prima Donna in Benjamin Disraeli's novel *Vivian Grey*.

3. The Banking Crisis

Rumours abounded. Few could believe what they were hearing. It just couldn't be true. The bedrock of Chichester society had collapsed. Ridge, Newland & Ridge, otherwise known as the Chichester Bank, was no more. It had gone bust and hundreds of local citizens had lost their money. For some it was a few pounds while for others it was hundreds and even thousands of pounds.

> THE Directors of the above Company having adopted the suggestion of various friends promising their patronage and support, in consequence of the closing of business by the Old Chichester Bank, have OPENED a BRANCH of their ESTABLISHMENT in this City, and until suitable Premises can be obtained, business will be conducted opposite the Swan Hotel, in East-street.

Above: Announcement in December 1841 that the London and County Bank would open a branch in Chichester. Following the collapse of the Old Chichester Bank in 1841 it was essential that a new and much larger bank be established in the city and one that would bring with it total security from a failure through lack of capital. Following consultation with members of Chichester's elected corporation (often referred to as the town council), the London and County stepped into the breach. This was not, in any way, a bank similar to the Old Chichester, being a joint stock bank that had branches throughout the country. Initially, until it established itself with a new building, the bank was situated on the south side of East Street slightly further down than the present-day HSBC.

Right: Once firmly established in Chichester, the London & County moved to a purpose-built structure on the opposite side of East Street from where the bank had been originally located. This is the building now occupied by NatWest.

For a good many decades, the Chichester Bank, originally created in 1779 and acquired by William Ridge in 1809, had been the largest bank in the city, with its banking house located in East Street (now the site of Lloyds Bank). Trusted by all, it was a highly important asset, successfully underpinning many of the city's commercial undertakings. While banks of the early nineteenth century were frequently subject to bankruptcy proceedings, the Ridge family bank seemed capable of weathering any storm. So confident were those who kept their money in the Chichester Bank that few, if any, attempted to remove their savings when, in November 1828, a considerable loss was announced. This was the occasion of the Chichester Bank's London agent, the banking house of Fry & Chapman, going into liquidation and taking with it a sum of money belonging to the Ridge family bank. Some newspaper reports suggested it was as much as £49,000 but the sum was later proved to be less. Often, the mere rumour of a loss even half this amount was sufficient for a damaging run on most banks, but the Chichester Bank had survived through the confidence of its investors.

DID YOU KNOW?

The value of money has changed considerably since the early to mid-nineteenth century. To get a notion of how cumulative UK inflation has affected the value of the pound, it can be suggested that the pound of that period in time has now (2015) a value of approximately £90. Thus, the initial reported losses of the Chichester Bank, given as £49,000 would be the equivalent, in today's money, of £4.4 million. The later quoted annual salary of William Ridge would now amount to £72,000 and that of William Newland would be £54,000. As head clerk, William Williams received a somewhat more miserly £11,700. At the time of its collapse, the Chichester bank had in circulation notes to the value of £13,000 (approximately £1.17 million in today's money) and an accumulated debt of between £120,000 and £150,000 (approximately £10.8 million to £13.5 million).

But, as it turned out, this confidence was misplaced. Mismanagement, inadequate accounting procedures and a lack of overall regulation led to the Chichester Bank spiraling towards disaster. While attempts were made to place the blame on the cashier and head clerk, there can be little doubt that it was the man at the helm, Charles Ridge, the senior partner who was the one at fault. He should have been aware that, over a good many years, the bank had simply been running at a loss.

Almost exactly thirteen years after the failure of Fry & Chapman's London bank, the Chichester Bank went the same way, closing its fine ornate doors in East Street on Saturday 13 December 1841. With no warning given, customers had fully expected the bank to reopen as normal on the following Monday at 9 a.m. Mystification could be seen on the faces of those who had assembled outside the bank on that cold wintery morning. Why hadn't William Williams, the chief clerk, opened the door? Where was

Right: The original London & County building, now NatWest, as it is today. Originally known as the Surrey, Kent & Sussex Banking Co., it became the London & County in 1839. Following various mergers and periods of expansion, the London & County became the Westminster Bank and eventually NatWest.

Below: Evidence of the London & County having once had a presence in Chichester is clear from this inscription over the door of the NatWest bank in East Street. The date 1836 refers not to the building but to the original formation of Surrey, Kent & Sussex Banking Co. in 1836.

Lloyds, through mergers and take-overs, is another bank with lengthy Chichester connections, these beginning with the Hampshire Banking Co. which had been established in Chichester from at least the mid-1860s. The site on which the building stands was also where the Old Chichester Bank, otherwise Ridge, Newland & Ridge, was once located.

William Goodeve, the chief accountant? These were the two men with which the public had the most dealings. Between them they could boast some fifty years of serving the bank's many customers. So long had they been on the front line of local banking they could put a name to the face of most of those who entered. Unlike modern banks, with their staff often seemingly distant, this was an informal family bank where savers large and small, were made to feel welcome. Among its customers could be numbered various local charities, a good many local shopkeepers and small farmers together with those at the top end of Chichester society, including the duke of Richmond.

By mid-morning, with the bank still not admitting any customers, rumours began to spread. This was a day like no other. All around the city small groups gathered to discuss what had become of Ridge, Newland & Ridge and, more especially, what hope there was for the return of the savings that many had in the bank. Some of the groups seen to be in discussion were a strange mixture, men and women who would not normally offer the time of day to each other. An occasional local correspondent for the *Sussex Advertiser* wrote of a 'sturdy mechanic' in deep conversation with a clergyman and a 'starched ironed dandy' with a sweep. Joining one particular group of four, the correspondent learnt that one had in the bank savings of £200, a second £300 and a third £260. As for the fourth, he personally had lost nothing, but had three sisters who had placed everything in the Chichester Bank, amounting to £3,000. Quickly miscalculating, for here we have someone whose mathematical abilities fell short of the mark, the correspondent added, 'three thousand six hundred and sixty pounds, thought I, gone at one fell swoop!' Leaving the party he turned for home to brood over his own misfortunes, for presumably the correspondent had also lost his own savings, going on to add, 'Chichester! Verily thou art the "City of Plague". Thy house of joy and gladness are turned into woe and mourning. Grim poverty skulks abroad in thy streets, and the hand of adversity is on thy inhabitants.'

The Barclays Bank building in East Street is on the site where the New Chichester Bank was once located, this the bank that was formed by Hack & Dendy but later came under the proprietorship of Dendy, Comper & Gruggen.

With no clearer picture of what exactly had happened, other than that the bank had folded, the mayor of Chichester, Dr Joseph McCarogher, called a meeting of the inhabitants of the city to pass a vote of confidence in the city's other bank, that of Dendy, Comper & Gruggen. This particular bank, created during the first decade of the nineteenth century as Hack & Dendy, with its banking house also in East Street (now the site of Barclays), was frequently referred to as the New Chichester Bank through having been formed some thirty years later than the Ridge, Newland & Ridge bank. In consequence of the Dendy, Comper & Gruggen bank being known as the New Chichester Bank, the Ridge family bank was frequently referred to as the Old Chichester Bank. It seems that the meeting called by the mayor was well attended and the vote of confidence duly passed, but of course it made not one iota of difference to those who had lost their savings. However, it probably prevented a run on Chichester's second bank and preventing others from also losing their savings.

Further rumours abounded throughout the week. Wednesday was a day of hope. Charles Ridge, the senior partner, had left for London over the weekend and had now returned. The belief spreading across the city was that a man of known wealth was ready to join the firm and that the bank would reopen on Friday. Come Friday, however, the doors of Ridge, Newland & Ridge remained firmly sealed, with the *Sussex Advertiser*'s local correspondent remarking that 'a duller or worse' day had never been witnessed. All now knew that the bank had been officially declared bankrupt, with nobody likely to receive more than 12.5 per cent of any money they had deposited in the bank.

So how had this come about? What circumstances had led to the failure of this much trusted bank and the loss of savings belonging to so many? As much as anything, it had been a lack of regulation. Start with the fact that at this time banks were allowed to issue low denomination notes that were freely circulated as currency and were supposedly backed by readily available assets held by the issuing bank. This was a state of affairs that was curtailed in 1844 when, under the Bank Charter Act, no newly established bank could issue notes, with exclusive note-issuing powers in England eventually falling to the Bank of England. However, with banks responsible for their own regulation and limited in the resources that could be called upon, the smaller country banks frequently became over-extended. In the case of Ridge, Newland & Ridge, matters were made more serious by improper accountancy methods that failed to show that the bank had become heavily debt laden over a period of many years. One might have expected Charles Ridge, the senior partner and the man who took an income from the non-existing 'profits' of the bank each year to have regularly checked the accounts to assure himself that the company was in a good state of health. This he singularly failed to do; it was later disclosed that neither he, nor his two partners, had checked the account books for a period of twenty years! Apart from the heavy losses sustained by the failure of Fry & Chapman, the bank was also failing to cover its numerous overheads, these including annual salary payments to the two junior partners William Ridge and William Newland, the former receiving £800 and the latter £600. In addition, Williams, the chief clerk, and Goodeve, the chief accountant, had also to be paid, the two of them receiving nearly £300 annually.

A further factor that possibly ate into the bank's ability to sustain itself was that of it being subject to fraud on several occasions. That it issued notes, these easily forged, may well have resulted in the Chichester Bank having to meet the face value of notes that had never been issued. More serious was a suggestion that Williams and Goodeve had embezzled large amounts of the bank's money, with both brought to trial at the Bow Street Magistrates' court in London. While nothing was proven, with both men subsequently released, the internal workings of the bank were shown to be highly inadequate. If any of the partners of the bank had attempted to earn their income by carrying out even a cursory examination of the accounts, they would have seen the substantial losses being accumulated. On the day the bank ceased trading, debts amounted to £120,000 with assets standing at no more that £54,000.

At one time Williams and Goodeve were held to be the cause of the bank's failure, a rumour running around Chichester that between them they had snaffled away some £5,000. Williams did not help himself by claiming that, on a number of occasions he had done wrong, but this appears to have referred to his inability to keep an accurate and easily decipherable set of accounts. Between them, these two men had complete control over the workings of the bank, with Goodeve taking responsibility for all cash and notes issued while Williams met payments on cheques and the receipt of money. Neither checked the accounts held by the other and no partner, until the day the bank collapsed, bothered to oversee the books. Due to inaccuracies in their accounts, made worse by their lack of training and non-standard methods of record keeping, it appears that the £5,000 Williams and Goodeve were accused of embezzling was no more than a series of accounting errors that had built up over the years.

The failure of the Old Chichester Bank was a disaster for the city, reducing persons of relative affluence to abject distress. Among them were Elizabeth and Nancy Fowler, two unmarried elderly sisters, one a cripple, who between them had £1,969 deposited in the bank and were left with not a shilling on the bank collapsing and were forced to throw themselves on the parish. Another was a farmer by the name of Smith who had £225 in savings and a borrowed sum of £1,000 for the taking of a larger farm. Both sums were deposited in the bank at the time of its collapse. The largest of the bank's creditors was John Kent, a training groom to the duke of Richmond. He had placed his entire life savings of £4,595 into the bank; this acquired from his work at Goodwood and intended to support a large family.

DID YOU KNOW?

In earlier times private banks, such as the Old Chichester, were allowed to issue small denomination notes. When the Chichester Bank sent bundles of these notes to Fry & Chapman, the bank's agent in London, these would be sent in two separate parcels on two separate occasions. In one package, with the notes having been cut in half, would be placed the right-hand side of the notes and in the other package the left-hand side. This was a simple means to prevent their loss by theft.

In December 1815 John Binstead, aged twenty-two, was executed in front of the Debtors' Door of Newgate Prison for forging a Chichester bank note to the value of £10.

Notes issued by the old Chichester Bank were used to convict a thief in 1824 who had stolen money being conveyed for a private individual in a box carried on the Portsmouth to London coach. The notes taken were numbered, with these numbers circulated to other banks, including the Hastings Bank. Later in the year, a certain Mr Tooth attempted to cash one of these notes at the Hastings Bank, with the cashier realising it was one of those stolen. Following a search of his rooms and with more of the stolen notes found, Tooth was arrested and subsequently sentenced to seven years' transportation.

Affixed to the Barclays building is a plaque commemorating the connection of James Hack, a Quaker, with the New Chichester Bank and founded on this same site.

4. The City's Greatest Benefactor

In October 1866, Dr Nicholas Tyacke, a senior surgeon at the infirmary and a member of the Royal College of Physicians with his own medical practice centred in North Street, made it clear that it was his absolute belief that there was something dreadfully wrong with the health of the city. As evidence, he revealed in one of the several pamphlets he wrote on the subject that, in the previous three months, Chichester had witnessed fifty-eight registered deaths of which fourteen were from diarrhoea or cholera and sixteen from fever of the gastro enteric type. As for the cause of what he considered to be such an unacceptably high number of deaths, Tyacke placed this squarely upon both a lack of clean water and inadequate drainage.

At that time, Chichester not only lacked main drainage but a good many of the cesspools within the area of the city were often positioned close to neighbouring wells and into which seepage was not uncommon. As for the River Lavant which flows around part of the city, this was nothing less than an open sewer while heaped piles of refuse from the city slaughterhouses, together with defective drains that belonged to these numerous slaughterhouses and associated piggeries, simply added to the problem. A particular health hazard was a large pool in a garden attached to the charity foundation of St Mary's Hospital which, for many years, had received the drain water and refuse of the neighbourhood. In a letter written to the *Hampshire Telegraph* in May 1852 and signed Omega, it was claimed that this pool by that time showed to perfection the ability to produce gas through it being 'denoted by innumerable bubbles oozing upwards continually'.

The Council House, North Street. For many years the town council resisted the introduction of main drainage into the city, with this policy overthrown in November 1892 when a majority of councillors favouring drainage came to be elected.

George Loader's map of 1812 showing the course of the River Lavant as it passed along the south side of the city. The Lavant during much of the nineteenth century was nothing less than an open sewer that contributed significantly to the city's health problems.

The River Lavant, now partly hidden, is still visible in parts of the outer city.

Two years earlier, Tyacke had provided evidence to the Medical Department of the Privy Council, the government's main advisory body on public health, as to the high morbidity rate within the city, with the Privy Council subsequently producing a report which recognised that the death rate in the city, which at that time stood at 22.7 per thousand, was not only exceptionally high but was above that of most metropolitan boroughs. Dr Edward Seaton, who took responsibility for compiling the Privy Council report not only expressed surprise at this appalling situation but went on to note that Chichester had everything that was normally associated with good health. He indicated that as a city it was 'well situated' and 'not over-crowded', having 'within its bounds even fields and open country, in which no large manufactories are carried on'. Seaton therefore had no doubts when he concluded that something was 'radically amiss in the sanitary conditions of the place'. From Dr Tyacke in particular, Seaton had learnt that diseases resulting 'from unwholesome conditions' prevailed throughout Chichester but were particularly prevalent in the poorer areas where housing was at its greatest density. In the words of Dr Seaton's report,

> The places about Somerstown, such as Cavendish Street, High Street, George Street and the courts running out of them, were the cases in which fever most prevailed, and in which epidemic and other diseases always tended to put on low types. In Cavendish Street nearly every house had its case or cases of fever, and in many particular houses in this and other streets fever shows a constant tendency to recur. Parts of St Pancras were hardly less bad. But no part of the city seemed exempt or any class of the population.

Quite naturally, Seaton, in listening to Dr Tyacke, gave considerable attention to the reasons Chichester, due to its ideal location and lack of industry, was one of the least healthy of cities in England rather than being one of the healthiest. To this end Seaton noted the existence of a regular cattle market that brought into the centre of the city thousands of cattle, sheep and other farm animals. The resulting accumulation of animal excrement in attracting flies during the summer also ensured the efficient spread of a range of illnesses of which diarrhoea and vomiting were the most frequent symptoms. It was to the lack of drainage to which Seaton devoted most of his attention, viewing the frequent use of the Lavant as a sewer to be a significant factor in the abnormally high morbidity rates of the area. Adding to this was that householders at a distance from the river were usually dependent upon cesspools that were nothing more than so many holes in the porous soil. Again, in the words of the Privy Council report as compiled by Dr Seaton,

> The liquid that flows into them being either absorbed by the ground beneath or overflowing and running into the soil nearer the surface. Out of other deeper holes in this porous soil all the drinking water is taken; these wells being so constructed that any fluid may percolate into them laterally. The whole city is thus riddled with holes – the deeper holes or wells being frequently within a few feet of the shallower holes or cesspools. Under such circumstances the frequent contamination of the drinking water is inevitable.

The elected corporation or town council, through it being the legally constituted sanitary authority, was held singularly responsible for this appalling state of affairs, seen as lethargic at best and criminally irresponsible at worst. As evidence of this, the report cited the council's Nuisance Removal Committee, a body that was supposed to hold regular meetings but had not done so for several years. As for some of the individuals who sat on the council, they too had a lot to answer for, with Seaton identifying councillors, as well as magistrates in the city, as responsible for some of the worst health nuisances. As for the response of the council's appointed Inspector of Nuisances, he was certainly aware of the failings of these councillors but was powerless to force them to take action, knowing that 'a more active administration of his duties would not be favourably regarded' by his employer, the town council.

The report was so shocking that its findings were soon appearing in a number of widely distributed newspapers including the *London Times* and *Reynolds News*. Both these newspapers drew a sharp contrast between a city in outward appearance that was all 'a tourist or visitor could desire' while on the inside 'full of all uncleanness'. *The Times*, in particular, reflected on the city's average of 200 deaths in any one year,

> They are bad deaths – deaths from gastric or typhoid fevers, with a great deal of sickness and invaliding from the same cause. Fever in some type or other incessantly haunts the city, and not merely the lowest parts of it.

Placed under so much pressure, it might seem that the town council would have had little alternative but to accept and act upon the findings made by one of the Privy Council's leading physicians. Dr Tyacke, who was also a member of the town council and a former mayor, pressed heavily for the findings of the report to be accepted and continued in his campaign to get the council to undertake a full system of drainage within the city. Reluctantly it seems, the town council did agree to establish a small committee to investigate the likely costs, with Dr Tyacke one of its members. However, it soon became clear that Tyacke's fellow members of the committee were completely against spending any of the council's money on drainage, concluding that other nearby cities, such as Salisbury, which had adopted such schemes, had witnessed no overall improvement in health.

With the committee eventually presenting a negative report that completely overruled any views put forward by Dr Tyacke, the council, aware that pressure was mounting did make one small compromise, agreeing to increase the number of Inspector of Nuisances that they employed. These were to be tasked with making house-to-house inspections to ensure that cesspools were not overflowing and that nearby wells were free of pollution. In addition, any sewage pipes still flowing into the Lavant were to be removed. This however, did not prevent the continued dumping of sewage into the river, with the council further agreeing to enclose the river as it passed through Eastgate, so reducing the stench, while deepening it at Southgate to increase, when the bed was not actually dry, the flow of water out of the city.

All this of course did little to assuage Dr Tyacke together with an increasing number of local residents who were demanding main drainage. Among Tyacke's many supporters was the anonymous Anglicanus of Chichester, who bestowed on him the accolade of a future generation likely to regard him as the city's 'greatest benefactor'. In a letter to the *London Times* that appeared in October 1866, Anglicanus had used evidence produced by Dr Tyacke on the cause of so many deaths in the city during the summer of 1866,

> What further proof need we that there is something radically amiss in the sanitary conditions of our city and who can doubt that an abundant supply of good water in connection with proper drainage is the only remedy and that it is of urgent necessity.

Fortunately, or so Tyacke possibly believed, one new weapon to get the council to take more radical action, now lay at his disposal – a newly introduced Sanitary Act

(The Sanitary Act, 1866). Here, in section 49 it was clearly stated that, following upon a complaint that a properly constituted local authority had failed to provide 'sufficient sewers' or a wholesome 'supply of water' then an enquiry could be instituted by the Home Office that could lead to a possible enforcement notice. Within weeks of the new law having reached the statute books, the home secretary in London received a memorial from thirty-nine residents of Chichester demanding that just such an enquiry should be undertaken.

Probably reflecting the Home Secretary's own concerns, given the publicity that Chichester was receiving, the request was not only approved, but an enquiry was immediately arranged and to which Dr Tyacke again provided evidence. He indicated that the worse forms of illness were to be found in the neighbourhood of the River Lavant but with further illnesses often associated with a large and offensive drain that took sewage from the infirmary. From G. L. Purchase, the city surveyor, it was elicited that the whole of the Lavant had not been cleared out for several years with filth accumulating in areas of the river recently enclosed, so negating one particular council initiative.

The outcome of the enquiry could come as no surprise to anyone familiar with the state of the city, the council required to introduce both a combined system of main sewerage and house drainage while also required to obtain a good supply of water. In addition, the council was also asked to remove the market from the streets, the accumulation of filth from so many animals regularly entering the streets seen as a further contributor to the poor health of the city. Despite the possibility of these requirements being enforced under section 49 of the new act, the council chose to reject the findings. Instead, it accused those responsible for the writing of this report of not only being incompetent but in having a secret agenda designed to create work for engineers now that the railway boom had ended.

Formerly one of the unhealthiest areas of the city 'The Shambles' or Crooked 'S' was once home to numerous crowded tenements; its inhabitants suffered an appalling level of morbidity.

Helping strengthen the resolve of the council in not carrying out the recommendation to introduce main drainage was that of a memorial signed by 467 residents expressing their total opposition to such a scheme. All were ratepayers whose main concern was that of cost. More important however, they were also the ones who were least affected by the city's high morbidity rate and would least benefit from the scheme through having property with sufficient land that allowed any cesspool to be placed well away from the house. Furthermore, many of them would also be employing servants to remove from the house waste destined for the cesspool. Opposed to them, and admittedly this included a number of more enlightened rate payers, were most of the doctors and surgeons of the area. In addition, but muted by their lack of influence, were the poor of the city, the ones who actually inhabited the more crowded tenements of Somerstown.

Through prevarication, partly helped by the town council agreeing to the removal of the cattle market to a new and purpose-built site on the east side of the city, the entire matter of introducing main drainage fell into abeyance, with Dr Tyacke still unable to make any headway. However, the whole issue was renewed during the mid-1880s when the ideas previously put forward by Dr Tyacke a decade and a half earlier were taken up by a new group of highly concerned residents who had formed themselves into an impromptu pressure group that began calling a series of local meetings. Within a short space of time they felt sufficiently strong as to put forward a slate of candidates to stand for council in elections to be held in November 1889.

Sitting council members were sufficiently alarmed as to call a meeting at the assembly rooms to lay out their case for not supporting the introduction of main drainage into the city. To a packed audience of carefully invited supporters, it was stated that Chichester was, in reality, quite a healthy city with the death rate claimed to be the same as Salisbury after this city had been drained. Given that the audience had already been carefully selected, it came as no surprise that at the end of the meeting, on a vote being taken, those agreeing that the town council should not adopt a scheme of main drainage gained an overwhelming majority. Just over a week later, a further packed meeting was held in the assembly rooms, this time to be addressed by candidates at the forthcoming election but with only the drainage candidates putting in an appearance. On this occasion, the vote held at the end of the meeting was one that completely favoured the introduction of drainage.

Despite the efforts of this new and vigorous campaigning group, their initial attempt at gaining control of the council and bring about a decision favourable to drainage fell at the first hurdle; none of their candidates managing to secure a seat on the council. Matters however, were to dramatically change over the next twelve months. By then, the ad hoc nature of the drainage party had transferred itself into a much more formal arrangement through the establishment of a Sanitary Association chaired by an existing member of the council, Alderman Smith, and having among its members several other existing councillors. With the declared object of spreading to a wider audience, 'the advantage of main drainage', the *Portsmouth Evening News* in December 1889 informed its readers that this newly formed Sanitary Association intended to take such steps as would 'promote the sanitary welfare of the city'. Seemingly also, their arguments were now beginning to win the day, even securing a victory in the council chamber when a scheme for draining the city at a cost of £21,000 won a majority of two, this resulting from a number of non-drainers switching sides.

However, the end of the affair had not yet been reached. In the election of November 1891, the voting rate payers, the more affluent residents of the city, voted overwhelmingly against the draining lobby, ousting four 'drainers' and returning all six of the candidates who had stood in opposition to draining the city. Immediately, the agreed scheme was abandoned and Chichester was briefly returned to the Dark Age. Gastric illnesses were invited to continue unchecked, with cholera continuing to take responsibility for an average of six deaths in any one year.

Bitterly disappointed in this last-minute failure to implement drainage, the recently formed Sanitary Association played their final card, resorting, as their fellow 'drainers' had done nearly thirty years earlier, to section 49 of the 1866 Sanitary Act. To this end, 451 Cicestrians signed a petition that accused the council of defaulting on their duty to provide proper sewers for the city. In response, a second inquiry under the terms of the act was opened, with evidence heard in Chichester in June 1892. The council, or at least those with a majority, railed against the expense which it was claimed Chichester could not afford. In addition one councillor claimed the city to be significantly healthy but was forced to admit that several of the cesspools within the city were, most definitely, fouling neighbouring wells.

The considered opinion of the Local Government Board as communicated in September was that the council was in default. Councillors were further informed that unless a distinct assurance was given that the council would, without delay, carry out an effective system of sewerage, then the board would issue a formal order declaring the town council in default and prescribing a time within which 'they should perform their duty'. With the non-drainers still in a majority, the threat was simply dismissed, with one councillor declaring that 'as long as the non-drainers have a majority on the council they have the game in their own hands'.

The 'Royal' West Sussex Hospital as it later became (but originally known as the Chichester Infirmary) was not a place where patients, during the nineteenth century, could guarantee an avoidance of ill-health. It was not unusual for patients to enter with one ailment and die from another contracted within the infirmary.

A distant view of the West Sussex archives office where many documents relating to Dr Nicholas Tyack are held. This would make an ideal location for a commemorative blue plaque as the area shown in the photograph was also once occupied by his family home.

However, sense finally prevailed, if not among members of the council, certainly among the rate payers. In the next round of local council elections, held in November 1892, matters were turned around once again when the non-drainers were completely annihilated at the polls, all six of their candidates including the mayor, Councillor Bostock, defeated. It was now, with the drainers once again in control, that Chichester was able to inform the Local Government Board that an effective scheme of main drainage had been approved, with the first outward sign of its progress being the laying of a foundation stone at the outfall works in Apuldram in October 1893.

By now Dr Nicholas Tyacke, who was in his eightieth decade, had retired both from the council and his medical practice but was no doubt keeping a close eye on passing events. The laying of the foundation stone at Apuldram could not have but caught his attention and while he was not listed as being among the guests present on that occasion, one feels sure that he would have been there, if not in body, certainly in mind. Tyacke, a churchwarden of St Bartholomew's (his local parish church), a trustee of the Oliver Whitby School and President of the South-East branch of the British Medical Association, is buried in the city cemetery at Portfield, having died on 7 May 1900. Rightly deserving the epitaph 'the city's greatest benefactor', he has no other memorial than the Portfield gravestone. But of anyone, he is certainly deserving of a memorial that should be placed somewhere in the city by the now far more enlightened Chichester City Council. Hopefully this will come about one day.

DID YOU KNOW?

In 1865 the *London Times* described Chichester to be as unhealthy a place to live as the crowded tenements of 'Gray's Inn Lane or Seven Dials'.

Of the city infirmary, *The Times* in 1865 pointed out that there was a great chance of patients dying in the Chichester Infirmary 'not of the disorders they brought in there, but of diseases contracted within the place itself'.

5. Déjà Vu

On the evening of Friday 4 October 1872 the centre of Chichester came close to total destruction when a warehouse situated between East Street and North Pallant was engulfed in flames. Only one factor prevented what would otherwise have been an assured disaster –the weather. It was early autumn with temperatures to match while a recent fall of rain also helped in preventing the flames from spreading too far from the original source of the fire. Even more important, it was a calm day almost free of wind. If the fire had broken out in mid-summer or had been accompanied by March winds, the outcome for Chichester would have been truly devastating.

The catastrophic fire of October 1872 was fortuitously confined to properties in this area of East Street.

Shops on the opposite side of East Street were also damaged, but not through the spread of the fire but the effects of exploding cartridge shells.

Putting the element of fortuity to one side, another clear certainty that emerged from the events of that evening was that the city's fire service – overseen and controlled by the elected corporation (the town council) – was not up to the task. Not only did the local brigade lack a sufficient number of men to carry out the duties of fighting a large fire but the equipment it was using was old and unreliable, one of the engines having been purchased second-hand some thirty years earlier. Not helping matters on that desperate evening was that of the crew of the larger of the two engines taking twenty minutes to arrive, becoming lost in the jumble of side streets that existed in the Pallants at that time.

It was the large warehouse at the back of Halsted's ironmonger's shop in East Street that was the source of the fire, a building that was best approached through the Pallant. Here were stored large amounts of combustible material, including three barrels of benzene. This was a petrol-like substance used in domestic lamps and which had to be used with great care. A flaming taper, necessary for lighting the wick of the lamp, if mishandled could often ignite the benzene that would explode and shoot flames in all directions. This not only inflicted hideous burns on the householder but might lead to an entire house being destroyed. Retailers selling benzene, including Halsted's in Chichester, were required to obtain a special licence for its sale, this issued once it was proved that the benzene could be safely stored. In other words, benzene was a long-recognised danger and should really have been banned.

Left: The fire that started in a warehouse at the back of Halsted's shop was best reached by way of the Pallant.

Below: East Street, a busy thoroughfare that witnessed a number of major fires during the nineteenth century.

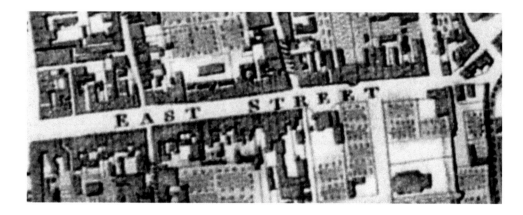

Imagine, then, the conflagration that broke out at the back of the ironmonger's store when three barrels exploded, one after the other; the resulting fire not only engulfed the entire building but quickly spread to neighbouring premises. According to one eye witness, flames shot 100 feet into the air. Consider, also, the panic that erupted among the few last-minute shoppers who were in this section of East Street. But what they didn't know, and of which the assistants employed in Halsted's were more than aware, was that the now blazing warehouse also contained 60 pounds of gunpowder stored near the roof together with paraffin and rifle cartridges.

Demonstrating the dangers of benzene was the assumed cause of the fire. Through barrels of the substance having been stored for a good many years, the warehouse had a fume-laden atmosphere. At 6 p.m., with darkness beginning to descend, an assistant apparently entered the warehouse with a lighted taper; this supposedly caused the initial explosion. The only problem with such an explanation is that of the assistant managing to escape – for none of the shop staff appears to have been injured.

Alerted by the three successive explosions, many Cicestrians were soon on the scene and providing help while other nearby hardware stores provided buckets for those collecting water from the nearest well. The worst was yet to come. Soon the flames had reached the gunpowder in the roof, setting off an even greater explosion, this heard over two miles away with the blast destroying the kitchen wall of an adjoining house. In turn, the stored paraffin also ignited with the liquid falling in flames upon the roof of yet one more house. Adding to this apocalyptic scene, which appeared more like Dante's imaginary inferno than the normally solemn cathedral city, was that of the rifle cartridges beginning to explode with bullets flying in all directions.

One of the neighbouring East Street premises affected by the fire was a jeweller and silversmith's shop belonging to Archibald Wilmshurst. With the help of his brother, whose printing works, Wilmshurst & Mason, lay on the opposite side of East Street, they managed to get Archibald's three infant children out of the top floor flat before beginning to move the entire stock of jewels, worth somewhere in the region of £3,000, to a place of safety. Wilmshurst the printer later recalled,

> We got great Buck baskets from a neighbour's; all my trusty hands were ready; a shop cleared opposite ready to receive it, and well-guarded, and now all that was wanting was to take the jewellery, etc., out of the glass case and window.

Doubtless Archibald Wilmshurst was particularly concerned about the safety of his stock, for only a few years earlier, in 1867, he had been subject to a trickster who had passed him a dud cheque before walking out of the shop with two expensive rings and a coral neck pin.

Eventually, having disentangled themselves from the back streets of the Pallants, the second of the council engines arrived. Working efficiently and assisted by a huge and willing crowd together with additional engines that had arrived, one from the barracks and another from Westhampnett, the fire was, after about two hours, brought under control. If more engines had been required, assistance could have been given by a further engine sent from Portsmouth. Upon the outbreak of the fire, the mayor of Chichester, fearing its imminent spread, had telegraphed Portsmouth, requesting that an engine be sent. This, together with several police constables who would be responsible for its operation, was immediately dispatched to Portsmouth railway station, arriving in Chichester around 7 p.m. Although gratefully received, it was decided that this engine was no longer required, the fire, while still burning, considered no longer a danger to the city.

This near destruction of the city centre had one important outcome – apart, that is, from the need to rebuild several of the destroyed premises. This was the realisation that an overhaul of the local fire service was required. Many now realised that those who manned the city's two engines did not have the training, equipment and numbers to deal with a major fire; if the conflagration at Halsted's had occurred during the height of summer, it would have spread so quickly that even the cathedral might have been endangered. Of course, one might have expected the mayor, or some other leading member of the town council to take forward any necessary improvements. But this was not so. Instead, it was left to a number of other citizens of status to take forward these essential reforms. For its part, the town council simply stood back and allowed these more dynamic individuals to begin forming plans for a new-style fire service – this one to be formed from volunteers and part funded by public subscription.

Within a few months a committee had been formed and had drawn up a clear plan that looked to recruit 100 volunteer fire fighters as well as the purchase of a new engine and the necessary appliances together with a portable fire escape. All in all it was a very serious undertaking as the volunteers would be expected to attend regular weekly training sessions and represent the city at various official events. In common with numerous volunteer brigades that existed around the country, members of the new city fire-fighting unit were expected to wear a uniform. For those of the Chichester brigade, this was to be manufactured under contract by Rawlins & Gale of South Street and to consist of a blue serge tunic with red facings and a black waist belt. As for the helmet, this was to be of leather with white metal ornaments.

Merryweather fire engine of the type purchased for the city in 1873.

Perhaps the most important date for the volunteers was Wednesday 14 May 1873, the day they took possession of their new engine. As for the old engine, this was now consigned to the vault below the assembly rooms. Arriving by train, the new engine was a Merryweather Paxton and described in the manufacturer's catalogue as 'a light country brigade or parish fire engine for twenty men'. Through the operation of manual pumps it could throw water 120 feet high and was drawn to the site of a fire either by horse or man power. To greet its arrival at Chichester station, the volunteers of the brigade, by this time some eighty in number, formed themselves into a guard of honour and marched with it through the four main streets of the city before finally taking it into the engine house in Eastgate. Throughout, large numbers of spectators lined the streets and the cathedral bells were rung. With many of the shops of the city also closed, the day took on the appearance of being a holiday rather than a normal working day.

Those who were long-time citizens of Chichester and of a certain age might well be forgiven for being overcome by a touch of déjà vu. Some thirty-five years earlier a volunteer fire brigade had also been formed in Chichester with a similar resolve that had resulted in the purchase of new equipment. Again, this had followed widespread uncertainty as to the efficiency of the brigade that was managed by the town council. As had also occurred in 1872, several enthusiastic individuals had formed themselves into a committee, laying down the requirement that volunteers should regularly train and also be eligible to wear a distinctive uniform.

There is every indication that this first volunteer brigade fulfilled all that was required of it, turning out promptly to a number of fires over the next decade or so. While specifically serving the needs of Chichester, it would sometimes be called to fires in some of the more distant villages. This was also a period of rural unrest, a result of farm labourers being made redundant because local farms were beginning to introduce mechanised threshing machines. On a number of occasions the brigade had to be called to douse hayrick fires that it was suspected had been deliberately started by discontented farm labourers. When operating outside the boundaries of the city, the Chichester brigade made a charge of £5, a sum normally met by the insurance company to which most farmers subscribed.

Eastgate, the site of Chichester's earliest fire station.

A flavour of Chichester's first volunteer brigade's ability to attend fires at a distance from the city can be gleaned from newspaper reports of a major fire that broke out in a Chidham farmyard. This was on the afternoon of 28 August 1839, sparks from a low-lying oven chimney having fallen on the thatched roof of one of the buildings in the yard, setting this on fire together with an adjacent barn and hayrick. Possibly not at the time, but nowadays this smallholding which lies alongside Cot Lane, and at that time occupied by William Kennett, is the apple orchard attached to Maybush Cottage. Upon the fire being discovered, messages were sent to both Emsworth (which had two engines) and Chichester for assistance. In Chichester, Edward Wolferstan, the brigade engineer who led all of the city's firefighting parties, quickly got a number of volunteers together and with four horses harnessed to the engine was soon heading towards Kennett's farm. According to a report in the *Hampshire Advertiser* (31 August 1839),

> so complete was every arrangement that the horses were put to the engine, and a body of firemen and other active persons ready and clear of the city and on the road to the fire before seven minutes had elapsed; and such was the rapidity with which it travelled that it was in full play on the fire in less than thirty-five minutes from the time of the alarm, having had to go more than four miles and a half.

Apparently Kennett and others heaped great praise on all those who attended the fire, with the *Hampshire Advertiser* adding one interesting point about the Chichester brigade, noting that they brought with them a number of leather hoses that could be connected together to form one long hose. This had proved a great advantage for 'if all the engines had been supplied with an equal quantity of leather hose to the Chichester engine the difficulty of procuring water from a distance would have been much lessened'.

The early efficiency of the first volunteer brigade did not last, for it came under heavy criticism during the late 1850s. Possibly the rot had set in as a result of the untimely death, from natural causes, of Edward Wolferstan, the engineer. He had been a member of the original committee that had created the volunteer brigade, with few others showing such commitment and enthusiasm for the success of the project. A long period of decline certainly followed Wolferstan's death, this eventually coming to a head towards the end of 1857 when the, then, mayor of Chichester, George Henty, decided to test the brigade's efficiency by calling them out, without prior warning, for a practice fire drill. In a near-farcical display of incompetence, it took an unbelievable length of time for the engine to be brought to the scene of the supposed fire. On top of that, according to the report that Henty presented to the council, those who brought the engine found difficulty in getting it to work, partly because they were untrained but also because 'there were holes in the pipes and tubes and the pump would not work'. To underline the point, Henty added that 'a pint of water would put a fire out as quickly'.

Fearful of what would happen if a major fire broke out in Chichester, members of the town council decided that enough was enough and that full management of the brigade must be returned to the council, with members of the Watch Committee given direct responsibility for overseeing its future direction. Among those who spoke at this particular meeting of the council, being one of its elected members, was Charles Halsted, proprietor of a certain ironmongers in East Street, who remarked on how important it was that 'the city should have efficient [fire] engines and men to work them'.

As with all things at this time, the town council proved highly parsimonious with the sums it was prepared to make available for improving the overall efficiency of the brigade. While repairs to the existing engines were sanctioned, it was determined by the watch committee that the city constables would now be primarily responsible for the fighting of fires. This a sure way of keeping costs down, given that they would be receiving no extra money for performing this additional duty. On the down side, of course, it meant that the numbers available for fighting fires was somewhat less, with the cataclysmic fire at Halsted's in October 1872 rather proving the point. On that occasion, there had simply not been a sufficient number of fire fighters to make an early impact on the fire, resulting in the subsequent establishment of a committee to form a new volunteer brigade.

As for the second volunteer brigade, the one formed after the fire at Halsted's, this got off to a rather poor start, rightly coming under heavy criticism when they attended a fire at Jenman's fish shop in East Street on 9 September 1873. Perhaps if the fire had broken out a year later the new volunteer brigade would have been better prepared, but fires being fires, they didn't always conform to the best interests of their inveterate enemies, the fire brigades. This unfairness on the part of the fire must be seen as the reason the brigade performed so badly on that occasion. Unless, God forbid, it was because the fire broke out at 2 a.m. and few of the volunteers could be bothered to muster.

This aside, it was the fire escape apparatus that lay at the heart of a subsequent tragedy, this a portable device of seven ladders mounted on a light carriage which had to be assembled before use. Unfortunately, those attending the fire were unable to connect it together, so failing to raise it to the second floor of the fish shop where Jenman and his young servant, Mary Ann Smith, stood on the window sill desperate to be rescued. On being called to the fire station by the ringing of the alarm bell, none of those familiar with the escape apparatus turned out, with nobody present understanding how the mechanism worked. Making the situation worse was that of it being dropped while it was being loaded on to the engine with part of the mechanism breaking. Upon the engine arriving, a botched attempt to raise the fire escape apparatus was undertaken, but the crew could only partially raise it. In desperation Jenman jumped and managed to catch hold of a rope attached to the apparatus, but his servant girl was unable to do this and fell back into the room. She was the unfortunate victim of this criminal display of inefficiency, for although pulled out of the burning building by volunteer Morgan of the Fleece Inn, a true Chichester hero, she succumbed to her injuries, dying in the infirmary two weeks later.

In time, and possibly as a result of the extensive criticism directed at the volunteers following their disastrous attempts to save lives in the East Street fish shop fire of 1873, they did get their act together. Over the next twenty or so years the volunteer brigade attended numerous fires in Chichester, their frequency of call-out being in the region of six to eight fires a year. Among the more considerable fires attended was a further major blaze at Halsted's ironmongers store in East Street in June 1893. This time the fire was in a store cellar where, once again, various inflammable materials, including gunpowder were being stored. In total contrast to the earlier bungled operation outside Jenman's fish shop, the fire was quickly doused, leading to the *Portsmouth Evening News* reporting that the brigade had set about their work with 'such alacrity that in a few minutes all danger was over'.

The former site of the Fleece Inn, this the home of one true Chichester hero who attempted to rescue a young stranded female from a burning building in East Street.

Policeman at Market Cross. A constable, at one time, could always be seen on duty at the market cross and easily found in the event of an emergency. It was here that Police Constable Peel was stationed and on hand to warn local residents that a fire had broken out in Edney's furniture store in East Street.

However, déjà vu struck again with a vengeance in September 1897 when the brigade's failure to tackle a major blaze led to the town council having again to step in and take direct control. As on that previous occasion, the fire which highlighted the weakness of the brigade was in East Street. The alarm was first raised by Police Constable Peel who was standing duty at the market cross. On hearing the sound of breaking glass he went to investigate and on checking the back of the shops in East Street, he discovered that a fire had broken out in Edney's furniture and upholstery store. Blowing his whistle to alert local residents, Peel also sent a man to the fire station where the alarm bell was immediately rung. Despite the prompt arrival of the engine, it proved of little use as, upon attempting to pump water on to the fire, the crew who had turned out discovered that the leather hose was rotten and therefore would frequently burst upon use. Only with the arrival of the barrack's engine together with an entire regiment of soldiers, followed by the engines from Emsworth and Havant, was the fire eventually brought under control but not before Edney's store had been totally destroyed.

Edney's furniture and upholstery store stood close to the cross in the centre of the city. In this partial view of the cross, Edney's Store (with the store name on the roof) can just be seen to the right of this late nineteenth-century photo.

The former site of Edney's spied through one of the arches of the cross. It was here, at his post at the cross that Police Constable Peel realised that a fire had broken out, having first to get to the back of the shop through an alleyway running off South Street.

It was the sheer incompetence of not regularly checking such a vital piece of equipment as the hose attached to the engine that led the council again taking direct responsibility for the city fire service. It was another déjà vu moment, given that this had also been the fate that had befallen the first volunteer brigade. In time, a possible reluctant group of elected councillors, spurred into action by a huge public clamour, splashed out on new firefighting equipment and recruiting a better-drilled force than the one that had been managed by the second of the two voluntary committees. Much more dramatic changes would eventually come about. In 1941, the Chichester brigade, in common with all other local authority brigades, was integrated into the National Fire Service to meet the needs of the war. While it had originally been planned that all these brigades would be returned to local council control, this did not happen. Instead, from 1948 onwards, the fighting of fires became a county responsibility, so leading to the creation of the West Sussex county brigade; a situation that remains as of this moment in time.

The inefficiencies of the frequently metamorphosed Chichester Fire Brigade resulted in the city being saved on a number of occasions by the somewhat more efficient barrack's fire engine and the timely arrival of large numbers of soldiers.

DID YOU KNOW?

Over the years Chichester has had three fire stations. The earliest was at Eastgate on the site of the original east gate entrance into the city. This was closed in December 1926 having been replaced by a much larger station on the south side of the cattle market alongside Caledonian Road. The current fire station on the Northgate roundabout and which includes the West Sussex fire brigade headquarters, was opened in November 1965.

During the 1830s and 1840s a voluntary fire brigade financed by the parishioners of St Pancras also existed and sometimes worked in unison with Chichester brigade. Among fires attended by both the Chichester and St Pancras brigades was the 1839 fire that broke out in the farmyard of William Kennett of Chidham.

Possibly the oldest fireman ever to serve Chichester was an eighty-seven-year-old who joined the reserve brigade in 1938, and who began his firefighting career in 1872 when he joined the volunteer brigade formed after the disastrous fire that consumed much of Halsted's ironmonger's shop.

Halsted's warehouse, the epicentre of the 1872 fire, was part of a much larger complex that included a foundry for the manufacture of farm machinery and other metal work. This was one reason the warehouse held so much combustible material, stock not just for the public but also the foundry.

6. Beer, Bribery and Bartering

The sight of drunken men, women and boys in the centre of Chichester might cause any modern-day politician to call for better policing and the ending of 'happy hour'; but not, so it seems, in 1830. According to an election handbill pasted around the walls of Chichester, John Smith, who in that year was seeking votes in an on-going parliamentary election, more than favourably viewed such scenes. Indeed, the handbill suggested he actually gloried in the sight of 'nineteen women and four boys and many men' falling about helplessly outside the Dolphin in West Street. Why? Because, so it was clearly stated, it had been Smith's money that had instigated this bout of mayhem. Making these claims, be they true or false, even more believable, was that of the handbill being apparently signed by the said John Smith.

This was all part and parcel of how parliamentary elections in Chichester were once fought – not with polite words but out and out insults or carefully or not-so-carefully veiled lies. Such handbills, which took to insulting an opponent, were common practice and were often referred to as squibs. Furthermore, with election laws of the early nineteenth century virtually non-existent, the number of voters limited and the secret ballot yet to be introduced, it was also extremely easy to manipulate the outcome of an

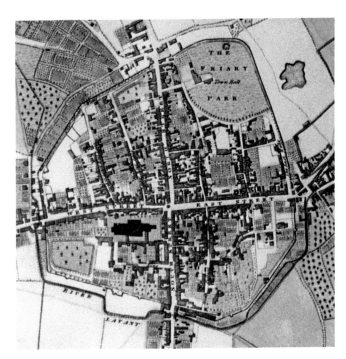

Elections in Chichester were once fiercely contested affairs. In 1831 it is recorded that there were 716 electors returning two members to parliament. At the same time Manchester, with a much larger population elected not a single MP to represent the interests of that city, Manchester being then part of the larger county constituency of Lancashire.

William Huskisson, a former MP for Chichester, and an advocate for railway building, is a name known to many as he was the first fatality in a railway accident, killed when he fell under the wheels of Stevenson's *Rocket*. He had been elected to represent Chichester in 1812, remaining one of its two MPs for ten years. His memorial is to be found in the nave of the cathedral.

The memorial to Huskisson in the cathedral makes a poignant reference to his untimely death.

election. Candidates not only knew how each elector voted but in Chichester could secure victory with a mere few hundred votes. As a result, bribery was common, with elections secured by those candidates who either flashed a great deal of money around or had some other hold over the elect.

However, of all those who sought election in Chichester, John Smith stands out as either one of the most maligned or a man with so much money that he simply had no hesitation in offering endless back-handers and carefully directed pay-offs. The son of a Nottingham banker whose residence was Dale Park House near Arundel, Smith had previously served for twenty-eight years as MP, much of this time representing the electors of Midhurst. In seeking to become MP for Chichester, it was suggested of him that he was there for no purpose other than to further the interests of the house of Smith. In that same election handbill, the one supposedly signed by him, it was claimed that his election would never benefit Chichester – other than through the money he dispensed – for it was not for the benefit of Chichester that he was standing. And here, possibly, there was a definite element of truth. Extending the Smith interest was obvious for all to see, with numerous members of his family having either served as an MP or were soon to be in parliament. In being elected to represent Chichester, as Smith was, it seems that he was doing no more than preparing the way for his son, John Abel Smith, who succeeded him as one of Chichester's MPs just a year later.

It was from the Fleece Inn, South Street, that Smith master-minded his 1830 campaign, issuing his own posters and election addresses but not the squibs that possibly laid open the truth behind his campaign and the reasons he was standing. These were presumably

John Abel Smith (1802–1871), who represented Chichester in parliament from 1831 to 1859, succeeded his father John Smith who had also represented Chichester.

issued by his electoral opponents. In an outburst of unrestrained honesty the sixty-three-year-old John Smith was alleged to have proclaimed,

> I am old and unable – and infirm and so on – but then I am as resolute as a Rhinoceros; and as to parliamentary duties, when it does not suit me to attend to them – I stay away.
>
> I am asked if ever I originated a useful measure during my long parliamentary career – I may have done so, but I don't recollect it.

Generous use of his money was a means he certainly used in attracting votes; bestowing on the infirmary, it was claimed, a generous bounty that came with a promise of more should he be elected. Subtlety, it was being suggested, was not his strong point, the spoof handbill informing Chichester voters,

> Though I have a long purse, I can hold the strings of it tight until it seems profitable to do otherwise – witness for me my first and recent gift of £100 to the infirmary.

To a woman who accused him of getting her husband frequently drunk he may, or may not, have retorted that once her husband had voted for him he would offer him no more beer – so problem solved. Many of the local citizenry, assuming they had a vote, got drunk at his expense, with Smith allowing alcohol to run free at the Dolphin. 'I don't want to see you sober at home,' Smith's ghost writer claimed, 'but to distribute cards for beer and see you drunk.'

On election day Smith gained, despite the dirty tricks played by his opponents, a total of 527 votes and more than enough to take his seat in parliament. Admittedly, Lord John Lennox, the second son of the 4th Duke of Richmond, gained 643 votes, but this was not a problem as Chichester at that time returned two MPs to Westminster. Once the result had been announced, the two victorious candidates participated in another Chichester tradition – apart from treating their supporters to more lashings of beer – that of being carried three times round the Market Cross before making their triumphal speeches.

Looking along North Street where crowds once gathered not outside the council house; here the results of parliamentary elections for the constituency of Chichester were announced. Nowadays, the results are delivered in a much more reserved fashion following a count that now takes place at the Westgate Leisure Centre.

Massive election-day crowds, such as this one assembled outside the council house to hear the result in Chichester for the parliamentary election of January 1910, was once a normal feature of city life.

It was the subject of beer that became a central topic of a further Chichester election held in January 1835. On that occasion many electors appear to have been unhappy at the quality brewed in the town by George Henty. Just three years earlier Henty, who owned twenty-five beer houses in Chichester, had purchased a brewery at Westgate and was now forcing each landlord of his various beer houses to purchase only the beer produced in this brewery. Given that there were very few beer houses outside of the ownership of George Henty and that the beer was not to the taste of many Cicestrians, it naturally caused a bit of a furore. Most serious was an election leaflet that circulated throughout the city that sought the support of the various candidates in breaking this monopoly. It did nothing to harm Henty's business enterprise which continued to grow, but the candidate the Henty family was supporting for the western division of Sussex, and which included voters in Chichester, failed to achieve election.

It was also the election of 1835 that demonstrated another peculiar aspect of Chichester elections in those years, that of ceremonial processions parading through the city in

Local councillors in Chichester were also local celebrities. On this occasion, Councillor Apps, who was also headmaster of a local school, has been invited to open a confectioners shop in the Hornet. Councillor Apps was first elected to represent East Ward in 1899.

CHICHESTER' BY-ELECTION

(Rec. 11.45 a.m.) RUGBY, May 19. Lieutenant-Commander Joynson-Hicks (Conservative National) received 15.634 votes in the Chichester by-election, against 10,564 by Flight-Lieutenant Kidd (Independent National) and 706 by Mr. Tribe (Independent).—B.O.W.

How a dominion newspaper, the *Wellington Evening Post*, announced the result of the 1942 Chichester by-election.

support of particular candidates. Early on the morning of 13 January, Lord George Lennox, again seeking election, having left Goodwood House, entered East Street accompanied by twenty carriages, 'upwards of 500 persons' on horseback (mostly 'opulent farmers') together with a juvenile party mounted on thirty-four ponies and numerous persons on foot. The ponies, apparently, were all decorated with orange ribbons, this the colours of the Whig party in Chichester and of which Lennox was a supporter, while the band of the Royal Sussex Militia played appropriate music.

Another, but slightly later feature of elections in Chichester was that of packed and rowdy election meetings. This was especially so after 1867 when the franchise was widened and most men in Chichester (but not women) had the vote and began attending such meetings. It was not unusual for the corn exchange to be completely packed out. The election of 1906, in which the Liberals were serious contenders for winning what was now being seen as a safe Conservative seat, saw some of the rowdiest of political meetings. A meeting held by the Liberals at the corn exchange in January of that year saw large numbers rushing into the meeting once the doors had been thrown open, among them many who opposed the Liberals. Within a few minutes, with the hall still only half full, and to prevent the continuation of this 'ugly rush' the doors were jammed shut, leaving 2,000–3,000 outside. Nevertheless, according to the *Chichester Observer*, 'the uproar inside the building was almost as great as that outside'. This made it very difficult for the platform speakers, each of whom was shouted down. At one point, a stone came crashing through one of the windows, while a firework was also set off within the hall. Eventually, the meeting had to be called to a halt, this on the instigation of the police, with the superintendent of the Chichester constabulary informing the chairman that the crowd outside could no longer be contained. Adding to the problem was that of the chain on the outside door having been broken with the likelihood of a large 'mob' gaining entry. Again, the *Chichester Observer*,

> The ladies were requested to leave by the doors at the rear of the stage, and as soon as they had gone the meeting closed.

Another Chichester election of particular interest was held in 1942. At that time, with the Second World War at its height, there was an agreement among the political parties that in the event of the death or resignation of an MP there should be no by-election in the constituency he or she had represented. Instead, only the party already holding the seat would stand a candidate, this to preserve the status quo. However, for many, this was seen as a Westminster stitch-up, with independents often forcing a by-election and taking on the big party machines with a surprising amount of success. In Chichester, following the death in April 1942 of Major John Sewell Cortauld, Chichester's sitting MP, the Conservatives, who held the seat, found that they were to be confronted by an independent intent upon mounting a particularly vigorous campaign.

The Conservative candidate, Joynson-Hicks, declared himself to be 'an out and out supporter of Mr Churchill and the national government', making it quite clear that in his view the prime minister and the government were 'prosecuting the war with vigour, skill, judgement and enthusiasm'. Against him were three independents, but it was Gerald Kidd, who made most of the running, making several forceful attacks upon Churchill and the way the war was being handled. Admittedly Kidd indicated his general support for Churchill, but seriously questioned the premier's ability to also be holding the position of defence minister. Instead, Kidd felt he should release the latter post to one of the many capable people around him while also demanding that more 'virile and younger men' should be brought into the government for the purpose of conducting the war more forcibly.

Kidd, himself, was a Chichester man. A solicitor in peacetime, he was the son of the late Dr H. A. Kidd, CBE, former medical superintendent at Graylingwell Hospital. Upon the outbreak of war, Gerald Kidd took up full time service with the Royal Air Force Volunteer Reserve (RAFVR), holding at the time of the election the rank of flight lieutenant (but serving as an acting squadron leader). Based at Dover, where he was part of a unit that linked the three services into a combined operational force, he might not have stood in the election if he had not directly witnessed the various inefficiencies that he believed were responsible for permitting the Germans to successfully transit *Gnesienau, Scharnhorst* and *Prinz Eugen* through the Channel almost within spitting distance of Dover. It was this that prompted him to stand in this wartime by-election, 'disgusted with the incompetence and lack of pre-planning' that had resulted in these ships completing such a daring escapade.

While the outcome of the election was a victory for Joynson-Hicks, it was far from being a conclusive result for a candidate who was supported by all three major parties. Of those who voted, 15,634 were in favour of Joynson-Hicks and 10,564 voted for Kidd. Indeed, the gap should have been much greater, given that Joynson-Hicks was standing in a strongly Conservative constituency and had behind him a party machine that provided him with committee rooms, loudspeakers, window posters and an army of canvassers.

By comparison, Kidd had very little. Even his committee room was created on the hoof, a private car that carried a large notice proclaiming it as a travelling committee room. Finally, the local county newspapers also appeared to be supporting Joynson-Hicks, most definitely giving the navy man more coverage than that of his air force opponent.

Providing this election with even greater interest was the presence of a fieldworker from Mass Observation, a social research organisation. Begun as a privately funded body, Mass Observation had been set up in 1937 to provide information on everyday life in Britain but was then being used by the government to investigate attitudes towards the war. Through the use of interviews and questionnaires, the unnamed fieldworker detected that in Chichester attitudes of the working class were undergoing a distinct change. Previously, in Chichester, members of this class, albeit relatively few in number, had been inclined to vote Conservative. According to the fieldworker, there were now clear signs of 'a shift in the working class vote away from the Conservatives' with those voting for Kidd often saying that he was 'more for the working class'. It was a perception that was to prove itself in the first post-war election, when the Labour vote not only substantially increased in Chichester but was retained at this new higher level in later elections.

It appears, from the fieldworker's research, that the Cicestrians themselves were also surprised by the narrow outcome of the election. Approximately 20 per cent of those asked by the Mass Observation fieldworker considered that Chichester was 'a Conservative town' and that it was pointless voting any other way. In an early form of opinion poll, 100 voters were asked whom they thought most likely to win. Of those offering a definite response, 67 per cent stated Joynson-Hicks, with 31 per cent suggesting Kidd would win. Compared to the outcome of the election, those believing Joynson-Hicks would be the winner was much greater than the vote he actually received.

As for their view of the candidates, these respondents considered Joynson-Hicks to be very much part of the establishment, with one remarking that he was 'a bit of the cathedral himself'. To this, it was further added that Joynson-Hicks had a manner and bearing 'that was pleasant if orthodox' and that he had an air of assurance. However, it was also considered that he might probably become 'pompous and self-reliant' in a few years. Kidd was possibly viewed as more of a local lad, with one respondent noting that, as the son of the well-respected Dr Kidd, many in the area had 'watched [the son] grow up'. His serving in the air force, although he was not allowed to campaign in uniform, was also looked upon favourably, one respondent remarking that 'he's an airman and they're reliable and have done a lot for us'.

One group of people, and they were among the disenfranchised, were the evacuees living in the constituency. Mostly from London, and having been brought to Chichester through being bombed out, it was noted that they had high levels of anxiety as to the future outcome of the war. This contrasted sharply with the permanent residents who, up to this stage of the war, had witnessed no direct bombing of the town. As to whom the evacuees might have favoured, this was not recorded. Finally, of the streets of Chichester, the fieldworker added one final point to the submitted report, that of these being crowded with troops and airmen, going on to suggest the city was three times busier than in peacetime.

SUPPORT CHURCHILL?
YES!

But free him from the ties of the Party Machine which :—
1. Ignored Churchill's own warnings.
2. Tried to destroy him Politically.
3. Landed this Country into war unprepared.
4. Stands in the way of Total Efficiency.

VOTE FOR
Flight-Lieutenant Gerald
KIDD

A flyer for Gerald Kidd's 1942 by-election campaign.

DID YOU KNOW?

Between 1660 and 1868 Chichester returned two members of parliament, the number reduced to one by the Reform Act of 1867.

Between 1812 and 1894 Chichester was continuously represented in parliament by members of the aristocratic Lennox family of Goodwood House. By those who attempted to break this stranglehold on the city it was known as the 'Lennox despotism'.

William Huskisson, one of Chichester's two MPs between 1812 and 1823, claims the dubious distinction of being the first man to be run down and killed by a railway engine. This was in September 1830 when he was run over by George Stephenson's locomotive engine *Rocket* during the official opening of the Liverpool – Manchester railway line. A memorial to Huskisson is to be found in the nave of Chichester cathedral.

7. A Factory at War

From the declaration of war in August 1914 through to its final conclusion with the signing of the Treaty of Versailles in June 1919 there was one man in Chichester who really had his finger on the nation's pulse. He, more than anyone else in the city and possibly the nation as a whole, had a clear idea of not only how the war was going, but the attitude and morale of those on the front line. Whereas those who planned the war might have readily available data on the horrendous number of daily casualties, they were less well informed on front-line troop morale.

The man for whom I make this claim was Alfred Ernest Cooper Shippam (1874–1947), and known to most as Ernest, a senior partner in the family-owned potted meat company that had a connection with Chichester dating back to the eighteenth century. Since that time, the company had expanded from simple retailing to that of processing, packing and wholesaling of a range of meat and fish products, with their potted pastes gaining particular acclaim. Among their customers, the Shippam Co. could boast the royal family and HM Forces, while in 1910 they provided canned meat products for Captain Scott's ill-fated expedition to the South Pole.

An interior view *c.* 1912 of the Shippam's factory under construction (photo courtesy of Princes).

The Shippam's factory as those who corresponded with Ernest Shippam would have known it.

The years immediately before the First World War had seen the firm undertake a particularly hectic period of expansion, this a result of Ernest Shippam and his four brothers forming a partnership in 1899 and using their combined finances to considerably expand the existing East Walls factory into a state-of-the-art meat processing works that was soon to be employing a work force of several hundred.

However, it is clear that Shippam's, which in 1913 was converted from a partnership into a limited private company, was very different to most other profit-making concerns. Ernest, and his four brothers, were not just concerned with securing a return on their investments but wished also to provide for the welfare of all those they employed. It was something for which the company, right up until the closure of the factory in 2002, was renowned. Not surprisingly, many in Chichester still hold the company in great affection, recalling its policy of paying a fair wage and looking after its employees and former employees when they fell on hard times.

Returning to Ernest Shippam and his depth of knowledge on the underlying spirit of the troops fighting the war to end all wars, this was gleaned from his one-time employees who had enlisted and were fighting either on the Western Front or further afield. In having regularly visited the East Walls factory and its attached retail shop, Ernest had formed a good relationship with the workforce and knew many of them by name. If they became ill, or he learnt that a close member of their family was suffering in some way, he would arrange for a box of groceries to be sent to the house, this accompanied by a suitably worded card. Consequently he was much loved and respected, with employment in the company much sought-after by young school leavers.

This caring attitude came very much to the fore upon the outbreak of war when seventeen of his 'factory hands', on 14 August, volunteered to enlist with the 7th Battalion of the Royal Sussex Regiment. To them, and later volunteers from the factory with a good work record, he promised that on the war ending, they could return to the East Walls factory while also providing each with ten shillings, this to be paid weekly and to make up for the difference between their previous pay and that which each would now be receiving in the army. It was a magnanimous gesture and one that he need never have made.

But it didn't stop there. Ernest made every effort to remain in touch with those who chose to enlist (or were later conscripted), receiving many letters from the front line. This he encouraged, always replying when it seemed appropriate and sometimes adding a request for further information, an occasional request for a souvenir of the war or for photographs of those employees who were now in uniform. Ernest also acted as a go-between, keeping those on the front line informed of the whereabouts and fate of factory hands serving in other battalions or regiments.

Come Christmas, and each of the enlisted factory hands would receive a reminder of their former lives with a boxed gift of six potted meat spreads fresh off the production line of the East Walls factory. To this, Ernest also added 500 cigarettes and, of course, a Christmas card. When he learned of one of the enlisted 'hands' being wounded and lying in a military hospital, Ernest would send a further 10s, this to overcome the fact of a wounded soldier not being paid an army wage while in hospital. In the sad event of a factory hand being killed, the Shippam's factory war memorial listed ten who were so lost, Ernest would send out notes of condolence to the family.

By the end of the war over 100 Shippam employees had either volunteered or were conscripted into the military, with thirty writing to Ernest. They were mostly the employees who had worked for the firm a good many years and, during that time, had built up a good relationship with the man at the top. Of the many others who joined the colours, the majority would have been short-term employees who most probably did not have a floor-shop familiarity with the boss, often joining the firm for a brief period before receiving their own call-up papers. It is certainly clear that, during the war, the turn-over of employees was much higher than in the peace-time years, with far more temporary staff being taken on to fill the places of those either enlisting or being conscripted into the army.

The names of many former Shippam employees are recorded on the panels of the Chichester War Memorial which was unveiled in July 1921. At that time, as this picture demonstrates, the memorial was located in Eastgate Square.

It was not just Ernest Shippam who was so charitably inclined, the other brothers and their families were equally compassionate, supporting wherever possible local Chichester charities. Shortly after the outbreak of war, Shippam Co. Ltd gifted fifty guineas and Ernest a separate £50 donation to the Chichester Relief Fund that had been established by the Mayor of Chichester. In reality, this was a local branch of a national relief fund set up by Edward, Prince of Wales for the purpose of helping the families of serving men and those suffering from 'industrial distress'. A leading member of the local Chichester committee was Ernest's wife, Mary:

> It was the frequent letters from the front that kept Ernest so well informed about the war; although I rather suspect that he really learnt a good deal more from face-to-face meetings when the former factory hands returned to Chichester on leave. Most certainly many of them made a point of visiting him and spending an hour or so in conversation. Here they would relate, it must be assumed, matters that would not have passed the censor's blue pencil.

Among the earliest of the letters received by Ernest Shippam was one from twenty-year-old Ernest Sidney Tilley, now Private E. S. Tilley of the 2nd Battalion 4th Company of the Royal Sussex Regiment but formerly a factory hand living in Stockbridge Road. One of his earliest letters was written from Horsham where Tilley had been billeted in a barber's shop following his enlistment six weeks earlier. In other circumstances, Tilley might have expected to have remained at the local barracks in Chichester for his initial training, but the high level of volunteering that had followed the declaration of war had exhausted available facilities with recruits by the hundred arriving daily. As a matter of extreme urgency, church organisations and residents throughout the county had been called upon

The Chichester War Memorial now stands in The Litten Gardens, St Pancras, having been removed from Eastgate Square in 1958.

to provide temporary accommodation. In Chichester, even the Olympic ice-skating rink in Northgate was being used for new recruits to bed down overnight. In the barber's shop at Horsham, Tilley appears to have fallen on his feet, telling Ernest Shippam that each morning he could get a haircut, shave and shampoo before going on parade. The only downside was that morning parade was 'seven o'clock sharp' not five-past as 'there is no five minutes grace like there is at the [East Walls] factory'.

From Horsham, where Tilley had undergone basic training, he was then sent to Newhaven and then Woolwich. At Newhaven, where new recruits often laboured on improving the defences to the harbour, Tilley reported that food was less plentiful than at Horsham where they had even got 'Shippam's Potted Meats for tea', but at Newhaven they had to 'fight for bread and jam'. His transfer to Woolwich, where he was one of the guards at the Arsenal, came early in the New Year, and by which time Tilley had learnt that others from the factory had now been sent out to France. To Ernest Shippam he wrote in May 1915, 'I hope they will return safely' while also noting that he had learned that 'a large number of wounded soldiers have arrived in Chichester lately and some very bad cases'.

The wounded soldiers to whom Tilley referred were among the first of many being brought back from France, the Graylingwell asylum on the north side of the city having been converted into a military hospital. By the end of that year, Graylingwell was to see

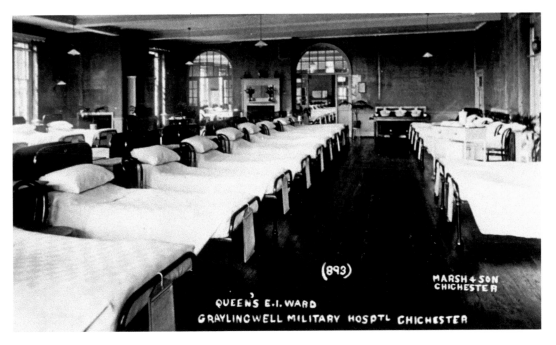

One of the Graylingwell Hospital wards. Graylingwell, which prior to the outbreak of the First World War had been a psychiatric hospital, was rapidly converted into a military hospital with hundreds of wounded soldiers brought here for final recovery. As part of his efforts to support the nation's war efforts, Ernest Shippam not only sent the factory's products to the hospital but also arranged for the more mobile patients to be provided with cars so that they could get out of the hospital and visit places of interest in and around the city.

The wounded and some of the staff at Graylingwell who cared for them.

Langley House in West Street which, during the First World War, was the residence of Admiral and Mrs Holland was, at one time, designated a hospital for the war wounded. This became unnecessary once the military had taken over Graylingwell. An interesting connection is the house is home to a large local GP surgery.

some 4,000 wounded passing through the hospital, having been brought there from the Western Front as soon as they were considered able to travel the distance. Tilley, himself, was posted to France later in 1915 and continued writing to Ernest Shippam until July 1916 when he was reported as 'killed in action'. However, there was much confusion as to his fate as his body was never recovered. His parents naturally hoped he had been taken by the enemy as a prisoner of war with Ernest attempting to find more information but without success. Tilley, who had been transferred into the 61st Division of The Royal Warwickshire Regiment, has no known grave, his name inscribed on the Loos memorial in France, the war memorial in Chichester and a memorial plaque placed within the main office and reception area of the East Walls factory.

George J. Farndell, another of the original seventeen enlistees, proved to be one of the most prolific of those who corresponded with Ernest; serving throughout the war he eventually reached the rank of sergeant. Seriously wounded in September 1916 and hospitalised in England, it was realised he had lost the sight of one eye, with Ernest offering to fund and take him to a London eye specialist. This was vetoed by a senior army medical officer, with Farndell sent back out to France where, shortly before the Armistice of November 1918, he again found himself in a military hospital following a further serious injury. A few months earlier, in July 1918, Farndell learnt that he had been awarded the Military Medal, informing Ernest that the citation was for 'services rendered'.

Another of the factory hands in correspondence with Ernest Shippam was Harry Francis Hall, also one of the original seventeen. Writing from Colchester Barracks, he asked if Ernest would contact their commanding officer to request that, upon further posting, the seventeen former factory hands be allowed to remain together. Ernest complied not only with this request, but a further one that Hall made from Shorncliffe where the group had been subsequently sent for further training, writing to Ernest on 22 October 1914,

> As myself and most of the other boys of our lot are putting in passes to come home this weekend, I thought I would write and ask you, if you would kindly write to Colonel Osborn to see if we could all come down [to Chichester] together.

Hall, who finally made the rank of corporal, was another who failed to survive the war, dying from the effects of mustard gas. This was in May 1915 with Hall buried at St Sever Cemetery Extension in Rouen. His name is commemorated on the Shippam's memorial plaque and also the Portfield War Memorial now located in the foyer of St George's church Rumboldswhyke. Farndell, in one of his many letters to Ernest suggested that Hall must have suffered greatly, writing that 'there is nothing more terrible than gas'.

Charles Tullet, another of the seventeen who had enlisted at the beginning of the war, wrote to Ernest in June 1916 of several factory hands being wounded, one by an exploding grenade. He also referred to trench life and 'having just been through three of the greatest bombardments ever known on the front since the early part of the war'. Earlier, in August 1915, Tullet had written to Ernest thanking him for a parcel of 500 cigarettes and which he had distributed to 'as many Chichester lads as possible'. To this he added, 'we always have a weekly allowance but the old familiar "Woodbine" goes down best'.

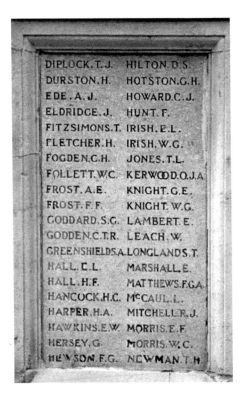

On this panel of the memorial are recorded the names of four Shippam employees: Harold Durston, Harry Fletcher, Harry F. Hall and Thomas Newman.

Left and opposite top: A further panel records the name of a one-time Shippam employee, Thomas Budd. Budd, a frequent correspondent with Ernest Shippam, was one of the original Shippam employees who enlisted in August 1914. His death, in October 1917, was much remarked upon by others who were writing to Ernest while serving on the Western Front.

An often forgotten memorial to the fallen of Chichester is to be found outside the former church of St Peter the Great, just opposite the cathedral.

A further letter of thanks was sent to Ernest in December of that year, Tullet incidentally spending Christmas Day in the trenches, following receipt of a further gift of cigarettes. Unfortunately, Tullet was a non-smoker, something we learn from Tullet's uncle who, in a letter to Ernest, wrote that his nephew was too embarrassed to say so, but asked that instead of cigarettes Ernest might send 'a few of your potted meats instead'. Tullet, himself, was wounded in July 1916 and while recovering in Rusthall Hospital, Tunbridge Wells, was sent a 10s gift. On that occasion, Ernest also made a point of visiting Tullet's grandmother who lived in Chichester.

Frederick Voller, one of the later employees to enlist, while in a military hospital in Newcastle-on-Tyne, provided this rather harrowing description of how he received a serious wound to his left arm,

It was terrible, they just put the machine gun on our wounded. I must think myself lucky I got back without being hit again.

To this, Voller added,

Remember me to all the boys that is still with you, I shall be glad to get back to work, it will be a big change. I shall like to see all the boys again.

News that some of their comrades had been killed was circulated with much sadness among the Shippam employees. Voller, in October 1917, having now returned to the trenches, in a letter thanking Ernest for the 'smokes' he had received, wrote of having learnt that Thomas William Budd and Richard Hewson (both 14 August enlistees) had been killed,

I was sorry to hear that, I have had my best mate killed, and he has no parents, he has only a brother and sister, I feel sorry for them.

A. F. Turner, a drummer in the Royal Sussex Regiment, in a letter to Ernest also referred to the loss of Thomas Budd,

I think it was hard luck about Tom Budd after being out here so long and he was only back off leave a little while, but I think most of the lads from the factory have been very lucky.

Budd, who came from Somerstown, was another who had corresponded with Ernest, having been writing to him since the beginning of the war. Aged twenty at the time of his death, Budd was killed in action on 3 October 1917 with his grave in Monchy British Cemetery.

George Baker, a factory hand who enlisted later in the war briefly returned to Chichester during the Christmas period 1917. Having been gassed, he had spent several months in an Edinburgh military hospital and his visit to Chichester was a result of being permitted a period of leave before returning to the front. This allowed Baker to visit the factory, later writing to Ernest,

Things are not like they used to be in pre-war days, when us chaps were there, but I hope the time will come again when it will be back to old times, I for one will be pleased to see the old firm, I did my best once for the interest of your name, and I would do so again.

In an earlier letter of June 1916, Baker had referred to the factory and how, with another former factory hand, they talked about the differences 'between the work there and out here'.

Another of the later enlistees, Private C. Hackett of the 12th Battalion, Royal Sussex Regiment, joined the army at the age of eighteen. He had been employed as a cutter boy, which meant he was responsible for wiping any surplus paste from the top of the jars with a muslin cloth. On receiving his Christmas 1917 gift of eight potted meats, Hackett reflected on those earlier times at the factory, telling Ernest that his gift made him think 'of the time when I used to wipe them off and I only wish I was doing it now but there comes a day when we shall all come back to the factory'. As always he signed himself off as 'your work boy Hackett' with Ernest playfully reminding the young lad that while he had worked at the factory he would frequently 'grouse' about the tasks he was given.

The signing of the Armistice allowed Ernest to keep his earlier promise that those who had enlisted would be given back their old jobs upon the war ending. This was good news for the surviving factory hands, as it meant that in having a definite job, those who had enlisted early would be eligible for early demob. All Ernest had to do was to inform the authorities in writing, naming the men concerned and adding his own signature. In this way the surviving August 1914 enlistees who had served in France were quickly in possession of travel passes and on their way back to Chichester. Others would also follow, with not a deserving worker failing to be offered his old job. One of the last to return was William Hilton, a factory hand who had been sent to the Dardanelles. He was still in the Middle East in January 1919, recovering from malaria in the military hospital of Basra. As with many of his fellow workers, he had kept Ernest informed of passing events, writing of how they had all been 'more than pleased upon the Turks surrendering' for we had been 'after them hot and strong'. On being asked by Ernest if he still wished to return to the factory he had replied with obvious eagerness, 'yes sir I am longing to get back and if you will get me out of the army I will be very much obliged to you'.

In total, some fifty ex-servicemen were eventually to be employed in the factory following the ending of the war – truly proving Ernest Shippam to be a man of his word.

In July 1924 the East Walls Shippam's factory was honoured by Queen Mary, the wife of George V, who paid the factory a visit and who made a point of meeting the many employees who had returned to their old jobs upon the ending of the war (photo courtesy of Princes).

Ernest Shippam photographed alongside Queen Mary (photo courtesy of Princes).

Shippam Co. Ltd was not simply a place of work but also a way of life for its employees. The young footballers in this photograph of the Shippam's Athletic Football Club would have been the sons of some of those employees who had served in the First World War and who had corresponded with Ernest.

DID YOU KNOW?

While Ernest Shippam had been busily corresponding with his 'factory hands' during the war there was one person, on the front line, from whom he received no correspondence but would have been desperate to gain news. This was an elder sister, Margaret Ann, who had taken Holy Orders before the outbreak of the war and was in a convent in Belgium. Throughout the entire war she was cut off from her family, living almost within sight of the German trenches, only returning to Chichester in December 1918 to spend Christmas with her family.

Following the war, the Shippam Co. continued to prioritise the welfare of its workers, introducing an employee bonus system, a staff clubhouse together with a profit-sharing scheme and a private pension scheme together with health insurance. All this was well ahead of its time.

Visitors to the East Walls factory would often comment on a pile of wishbones – several hundred thousand – with more added each day. Each visitor could take one as a good-luck token of their visit.

Tradition has it that if a Shippam employee was thought to have taken strong liquor at lunchtime it was demanded that they say, 'Shippam's Chichester Sausages'. If they were unable to say this they would then be reprimanded. As for the Chichester sausage, known as 'the celebrated Chichester sausage', this, for many years, was one of Shippam's best-selling products.

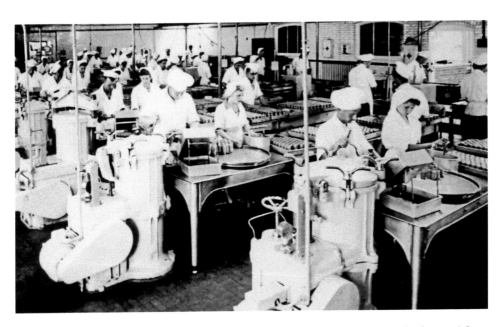

It was not until the Second World War that Shippam first employed women in the factory (photo courtesy of Princes).

A 1950s sample display of products (photo courtesy of Princes).

To help keep the name alive a newly constructed road close to the old factory site has had the name Shippam bestowed upon it.

The old Shippam's clock which once marked the site of the factory was removed when the factory was closed but was returned to its former site following public demand.

8. The Home of Crime Fiction

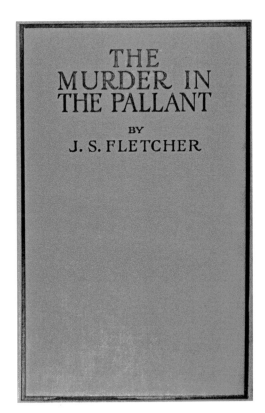

THE
MURDER IN
THE PALLANT

BY

J. S. FLETCHER

A flurry of detective novels during the early years of the twentieth century placed the city of Chichester at the heart of crime fiction. *The Murder in the Pallant* could be set nowhere else other than the heart of the city.

What was Chichester really like during the early part of the twentieth century? How did Cicestrians view the city and how did they go about their everyday lives? These are questions that are difficult to answer; rarely do individuals write or talk about matters that at the time would appear mundane and of little interest to others. But if the mundane can be part of something that is exciting, then it will be recorded in some way.

And this is exactly what happened to Chichester during the 1920s.

Two writers of crime fiction, Joseph Smith Fletcher and Victor Lorenzo Whitechurch, in having turned their gaze upon the city, helped uncover the hidden secrets of everyday life. It was a time when Chichester was a home – if not the home – of crime fiction. While writing of missing bankers, fraudsters and murderers in Chichester, they described the city in such a unique and unforgettable way that the reader might have stepped on board a very real-time machine. In these books the reader is actually there, penetrating the inner depths and thoughts of everyday people.

The front cover of Joseph Smith Fletcher's *The Lost Mr Linthwaite* depicts a publicity campaign mounted in Chichester to discover the whereabouts of a lost uncle last seen in the centre of the city.

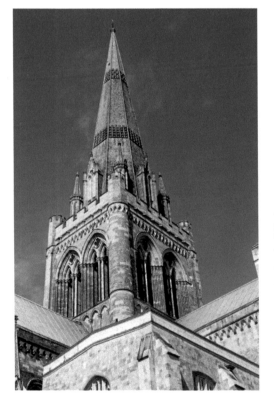

Another writer of crime fiction set in Chichester was Victor Lorenzo Whitechurch. In comparison with Fletcher, he had a much closer association with the city having attended the diocesan theological college. In his semi-fictional autobiography, *Concerning Himself: The Story of an Ordinary Man*, Whitechurch refers to his time as a child in Chichester and being able to 'catch a glimpse of the tall spire of the cathedral' when he drew close 'to one of the three windows' of the house where he used to live.

In their day Fletcher and Whitechurch were as famous as Agatha Christie and Arthur Conan Doyle, with book stalls throughout the country crowded with their much sought-after novels. Whitechurch had the strongest Chichester connection, receiving his early education in the city while going on to attend the diocesan theological college which was also in Chichester. His subsequent ordination in 1891 as a Church of England curate admittedly took him away from the city, but he made frequent returns to visit both family and friends. Fletcher, by contrast, had a much weaker association with the city, knowing it more as a visitor than a resident. In fact, Fletcher was born in Halifax, only moving to the south of England in later life when he took up residence in Dorking. Very much a full-time writer, Fletcher combined an early training in law with a later career in journalism to provide plots for over 200 novels.

That Whitechurch should set so many of his books in Chichester is relatively easy to answer – familiarity. Having strong connections with the city, this made it easy for him to integrate Chichester into a number of his stories. Furthermore, the cathedral and the clergy usually also make an appearance, this ensuring that Whitechurch could draw on detail that he knew to be totally accurate. There is considerably less certainty as to why Fletcher should set several of his tales in the city, given that he never resided here. Perhaps though, and given that his books sold particularly well in the United States, it

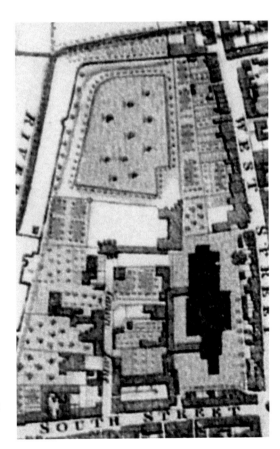

Whitechurch, who served the Anglican Church for much of his life, was particularly familiar with those who lived in and around the cathedral close – an area little changed from the days of George Loader's survey of 1812.

was because Fletcher viewed Chichester as quintessentially English. This comes out most clearly in the following passage from one of his earliest Chichester novels, *The Paradise Mystery*, released in the States in 1920 and which features a group of American tourists. Incidentally, in common with Whitechurch, Fletcher rarely chooses to refer to Chichester by name, referring to it as Wrychester, Selchester or Redminster,

> American tourists, sure appreciators of all that is ancient and picturesque in England, invariably come to a halt, holding their breath in a sudden catch of wonder, as they pass through the half-ruinous gateway which admits to the close of Wrychester.

Just a few lines further on, Fletcher adds,

> In morning, as in afternoon, or in evening, here is a perpetual atmosphere of rest; and not around the great church alone, but in the quaint and ancient houses which fence in the Close. Little less old than the mighty mass of stone on which their ivy-framed windows look, these houses make the casual observer feel that here, if anywhere in the world, life must needs run smoothly.

A further general flavour of the city, under the guise of Selchester, is provided by Fletcher in a further Chichester novel, *The Murder in the Pallant*, published in 1927,

> Selchester, although a cathedral city and the largest town in a quiet corner of a purely agricultural county, is so small a place that all its principal inhabitants are known to each other, if not by name at any rate by sight. Some, to be sure, are better known than others; there are always degrees of knowledge in this sort of thing. But a Selchestrian would tell you that certain personages and people of the city were known to everybody not only by sight but by name – such were the bishop, the dean and the great ecclesiastical functionaries; the mayor, aldermen, councillors, the civic officials and some other folk who, from having been there always and being seen constantly, were as familiar as the spire of the cathedral or the statues of the market cross.

In *The Lost Mr Linthwaite*, published in 1927, it is again Selchester, but there can be little doubt that it is to Chichester that Fletcher refers,

> Selchester was a very small town, divided into four segments by two main streets, one of which ran due south and north, the other due east and west; he was aware from an old map which hung in his bedroom at the Mitre, that it was enclosed by an ancient wall, running round it in an almost perfect circle.

The 'he' in this passage is Richard Brixey, the nephew of the Mr Linthwaite of the book's title, and who mysteriously disappears while on a visit to Chichester. The Mitre, where both Linthwaite and Brixey take rooms is, almost certainly, The Dolphin and Anchor Hotel in West Street.

Whitechurch, because of his long-term residence, is particularly good when it comes to drawing out some of the hidden quirks of the city, such as the distaste that many of the householders had for the numbering of their houses. This is an observation he makes following a highly accurate description of one particular property in Priory Road (which he renames Priory Street) that appears in *Mixed Relations* published in 1929,

> Priory Street was characteristic of a cathedral city. A narrow, quiet thoroughfare, with its houses by no means built 'according to plan'. On one of its sides, for instance, a big, Georgian structure, quite imposing, followed by half a dozen tiny houses, flanked again by a good sized one.
>
> No. 32 was one of these larger houses. Three steps led up to a front door flanked by pillars supporting a small portico, beneath which one entered a wide passage hall, with rooms – good rooms – on either side. And one of its surprises – which is shared

The Dolphin Hotel in West Street makes several appearances in the Chichester mystery novels.

The house referred to in the following description closely resembles one of the houses in the road running alongside Priory Park: 'No. 32 was one of these larger houses. Three steps led up to a front door flanked by pillars supporting a small portico, beneath which one entered a wide passage hall, with rooms – good rooms – on either side'.

The unusual ostrich sculptures that flank the entrance to Pallant House were described by Whitechurch in *Mixed Relations* as 'a bird of some impossible kind' before adding that the building 'was always known as "The Dodo House"'.

with many other houses standing abruptly on the street in Frattenbury – was the delightful little quiet, walled-in garden at the back, from which one caught a glimpse of the tapering grey spire of the Cathedral over the red roofs of adjacent houses.

At this point Whitechurch explains that the residents of the city never referred to their houses by numbers but only by the name of the resident. That the house which he picks out bore the No. 32 was, he indicates, a recent innovation, numbers having just been introduced by the city authorities. Apparently it was still a sore point within the city, older occupants at that time refusing 'to recognise the existence of these numbers'.

Central to the doings of an American fraudster in *Mixed Relations* is the need to hire a motor vehicle, this being obtained from premises in North Street. Although not named in the book, Whitechurch may be referring to Reeves (No. 15 North Street) and which he states to be 'the principal car-dealer in the city'. He describes it 'as an imposing looking establishment' while further adding that it had a wide entrance 'leading to a spacious garage in the rear'. On either side of this entrance were 'large plate-glass windows, behind each of which stood a tempting looking motor-car'.

The cross, of course, does not fail to get a mention and is, indeed, central to the plot of *Mixed Relations* through a family of criminals who attempt to lay a false trail by having their car identified by the policeman who always stood at the cross. As one of the family puts it,

I thought you'd appreciate it. You might even stop for a moment at the cross – there'll be no one about at that time except the bobby – and adjust something in your engine.

That a policeman always stood at the cross was something that went back many decades, even to the time when the city was guarded not by policemen but by the city watch. In doing so, it meant anyone who urgently needed police assistance (in an age before telephones or even before telephones were common) would know where one was to be found. Few photographs of the cross, in these earlier years, fail to include the regular officer standing to attention at the cross. As to the city being deserted at midnight, this appears to be another city tradition.

South Street is particularly well described by both Fletcher and Whitechurch. In *The Dean and Jecinora*, published in 1926, Whitechurch refers to a confectioners that stands

'At the further end of the little street he had entered stood an ancient, massive gateway, the entrance to the Episcopal Palace', this being Whitechurch's first reference to Canon Gate in *Mixed Relations*. Through Canon Gate, the length of this little street is viewed, looking along its length towards the gateway entrance to the episcopal entrance.

The deanery, which was erected in 1725, is central to the developing plot in Whitechurch's *The Dean and Jecinora*, and in which it is described as 'a big square building standing well back in its own grounds'.

Another building in the close and integral to *The Dean and Jecinora* is one described as being next to the deanery 'on the south side of the street'. It is the further reference to this being an old house having a gate that confirms it to be this particular building.

'Farther on, was a narrow lane on the right, at the end of which one could see the opening into the cloisters; while above all, towered the massive grey pile of the cathedral, surmounted by its tapering spire'. This is Whitechurch making reference to St Richard's Walk in *The Dean and Jecinora*.

just to the north of Canon Gate and where one of the central characters, Peggy, who is in search of lodgings, is informed by a house agent that there are rooms she might lease,

'Where is the shop?'

'In the South Street, about a couple of hundred yards down, on the right hand side. "Finch, Confectioner." You can't miss it. Quite respectable and very nice rooms upstairs.'

The shop in South Street described by Whitechurch in *The Dean and Jecinora* as being close to Canon Gate and possessing 'a large bow window commanding a view of South Street'.

Mrs Finch, a buxom little woman with a rosy face, at first demurred. Peggy, however, took care to state that she should be out most of the day. Then the good woman showed her the rooms. The sitting-room was directly above the shop, and possessed a large bow window commanding a view of South Street. Peggy expressed her satisfaction and settled the terms.

The shop, No. 20 South Street, is still there, just as described. At the time Whitechurch was writing it was, with a slight stretch of the imagination, a confectioners, being The City Cake Shop, but nowadays it serves a more demanding clientele, a specialist jeweller's shop that trades under the name of Ebony Jewellers Ltd.

South Street also appears in the opening pages of Fletcher's *The Murder in the Pallant*, a story that involves the theft of papers from a solicitor's officer in West Pallant. Before the crime is discovered, two of the main characters in the novel pass along South Street on their way to their respective offices. In doing so they pass the central post office, an institution which did stand in South Street until its removal in 1937 to its present location in West Street,

Your well informed native, questioned about them, would have told you that for some twelve or thirteen years these two had walked up that street every business morning at the same hour; that when they reached the post office in its centre each stopped, drew out his watch, and compared it with the big clock in the post office window, and that a few yards further on they separated, Mark Branson turning into that part of the city called the Pallant, and Louis Branson continuing his progress until he reached the office door further up the street.

Left: Referred to in Fletcher's *The Murder in the Pallant* is Chichester's central post office which, at the time he wrote this novel, was located in South Street. The building is currently the office of a travel agency.

Below: In the close, according to Whitechurch, 'lived widows of a type that never wax wanton and spinsters of a type who are too advanced in years to attempt to do so'.

The post office in South Street also receives a mention in Whitehead's *Mixed Relations*, this in reference to an evening stroll taken by one of the inhabitants of the nearby close,

There was an entry from the quiet close into South Street, and the post office was just opposite this entry. It was only a matter of a hundred yards, or less. Close to the post office was a cinema, already beginning to discharge its audience.

The cinema referred to was the Picturedrome but was renamed the Plaza just a few months after first publication of *Mixed Relations* in January 1929. The Picturedrome, which had first opened in July 1920, had an entrance in both South Street and West Pallant, with the one in South Street no more than a highly elaborate entrance squeezed between a café and an ironmonger, with the auditorium of the cinema set behind the two shops. During the late 1930s, and resulting from increased competition, the Plaza was completely rebuilt with a much more extensive South Street frontage. In time, the new building was acquired by the Odeon Group, with films continuing to be shown until 1960, with the building itself now a small supermarket.

SOUTH STREET, CHICHESTER.

A view of South Street contemporary to the novels of both Fletcher and Whitechurch. On the left, a little further along the street from Canon Gate, can be seen the bow window that commands a view of South Street while on the opposite side of the road there is an overhanging sign for the Picturedrome.

In Fletcher's *The Murder in the Pallant*, it seems likely that the murder took place not in the library but in one of these buildings in West Pallant.

In giving particular attention in his various Chichester-based novels to the cathedral area, Whitechurch has one of his characters approaching the close by way of Canon Lane,

At the further end of the little street [South Street] he had entered stood an ancient, massive gateway [Canon Gate] the entrance to the Episcopal Palace. Immediately on his right was a broad, stone-paved path, on one side of which was a row of beautiful old stone houses, half covered by Virginia creeper, and with neat little gardens in front. As he walked along the nearly deserted street he admired fine old houses, standing back, for the most part, from the road. Farther on, was a narrow lane on the right, at the end of which one could see the opening into the cloisters; while above all, towered the massive grey pile of the cathedral, surmounted by its tapering spire.

Generally, and what does come as a surprise, is that Whitechurch appears to have little sympathy with many of the residents of the close, regarding them, to put it politely, as elitist. This comes out in several of his books, with these descriptions having a ring of authenticity. Miss Duckworth, who appears in *Mixed Relations*, is certainly one who regards herself, through residence in the Close, as being on a much higher social level than that of the merchants, traders, artisans and labourers who dominated the rest of the city,

> The opinions which she respected were on a sliding-scale, so to speak. First class, those which emanated from the households of the Bishop's Palace, the deanery, and the official abodes of the archdeacon and canon residentiary. Second class, those which came from the abodes of the minor canons or other lesser cathedral beings. Third class, and ordinary, those from the world outside the sacred precincts of the close.

Many of the houses in the close, according to Whitechurch, were 'chiefly occupied by widows and spinsters', of whom Miss Duckworth was one.

> Not ordinary widows and spinsters mind you – not the widows of worldly mind who to quote the Apostle, 'wax wanton', or the spinsters who degrade themselves with golf or bicycles and other pomps and vanities of the world, but widows and spinsters who are in every way fit and eligible for the sphere of the close, who can say, 'my husband, the late canon', or 'poor dear father, we were only reading one of his sermons last night – a volume of them was printed after he died', widows and spinsters who have missionary boxes conspicuously displayed on the hall table, who attend the daily services with unflinching regularity, who are never absent from the Bible class of the 'dear Dean', and who are, in fact inseparable from the life (or shall we say, existence?) of the close of a cathedral city.

Another distinct community within the close were the minor canons who occupied the smaller houses of the close, these in St Richard's Walk. To Whitechurch they were,

> small fry who do most of the work in the services, but are not allowed to preach excepting at rare intervals – small fry who are useful in handing round tea at the dean's afternoon functions, and who in other ways are equally necessary to cathedral traditions.

Whitechurch's view of the close is further elaborated in his semi-autobiographical novel written towards the end of his life and entitled *Left in Charge*,

> In the close lived widows of a type that never wax wanton and spinsters of a type who are too advanced in years to attempt to do so, together with their respective daughters and nieces who attend daily services, filled altar vases, taught in Sunday Schools and otherwise showed themselves to be a species of high-grade Christian.

This, of course, is not dissimilar to the account already quoted from *Mixed Relations*. However, in this fictional autobiography Whitechurch chooses to throw his barbed arrows just a little further afield, noting that those who lived outside the close, but who could claim an association with those resident in the close, were equally as determined to use it as a means of raising their status within the city,

> The doctors prided themselves upon the fact that Bishops, Deans and Canons required their pulses to be felt occasionally. The principal lawyers held such offices as that of

the clerk to the chapter. The retired army and navy officers were precise in their views of their alliance of state with church, and never despised the Dean's sherry at lunch or the bishop's port at dinner. And the wives of them all vied with one another in getting invitations to garden parties and other dull festivities in the close. The doctor's wives would say to the lawyer's wife, 'Were you at the palace last Thursday?' Smiling sweetly because she knew all the time that the answer would have to be in the negative; and the lawyer's wife would recall the recent occasion on which she and her husband had dined at the Archdeacon's.

This desire to claim status through association was also to be seen among the traders of the city,

The rotund butcher, a member of the town council, would remark as he took an order for chops from the Mayor, 'I'm very glad to hear the Dean has lost his cold'. The grocer weighing out one's pound of tea with the air of a man whose mind dwelt on higher things, would confidently assert that the last sermon of the Canon in Residence was one of the most powerful utterances he had ever enjoyed. The florist would tell one confidentially, 'the dean has a large party tonight ma'am. We are doing the table decorations.'

Unfortunately, no more recent cleric has chosen to unveil his views on life in the Cathedral Close in quite this fashion. If they had, it would be interesting to know the extent to which such notions continue to exist in a city that is still – for the most part – quintessentially English.

DID YOU KNOW?

Victor Whitechurch's novel, *The Dean and Jecinora*, has been reprinted by the University of Chichester under the title *The Dean and his Double*. The 'Jecinora' of the original title refers to an off-the-counter patent medicine that intertwines itself into the plot.

Many of Fletcher's and Whitehead's titles are available in electronic format, the original hardbacks being almost impossible to obtain.

Fictional crime returned to Chichester in 2006 when *In a Monastery Garden* was first screened on British television, this part of the popular *Rosemary and Thyme* series. It involved the discovery of a body in an old garden in the close.

Modern-day crime writer Peter Lovesey has set some of his more recent novels in and around the city of Chichester.

Bibliography

West Sussex Records Office

Add Ms 1606	Wartime letters written to Ernest Shippam
Add Ms 22260	Election addresses and handbills, 1830
Add Ms 41258	Election addresses and handbills, 1812–14
MP2302	Early Banking in Chichester
MP 4065	History of Shippam Co. Ltd
MP4813	Hack, Dendy
Shippam Ms 5/1/1/1	Wage Book

University of Sussex Library

MOA 46/14/E	Mass Observation Reports

Newspapers

Chichester Observer, 1910
Hampshire Advertiser, 1830–1900
Hampshire Chronicle, 1772–1870
Hampshire Telegraph, 1799– 1900
London *Times*, 1830–1860
Pall Mall Gazette, 1865– 1899
Penny Illustrated Paper, 1861–1870
Police Gazette, 1773–1858
Portsmouth News, 1850–1920
Reynolds News, 1850–1900
Sussex Advertiser, 1746– 1867
Sussex Agricultural Express, 1857–1954
Wellington Evening Post, 1942

Printed Non-fiction

Berriman, Andrew, *'Squibs' The 1830 Chichester Election Campaign* (Chichester Local History Society, 2015)

Fleming, Lindsay, *The Little Churches of Chichester: St Peter, North Street; St Olave, North Street; St Andrew, Oxmarket; All Saints in the Pallant, etc* (Chichester Papers. no. 5, 1957)

Hussey, Revd Arthur, *Notes on the Churches in the Counties of Kent, Sussex and Surrey* (London, 1852)

Jordan, S., *Fifty Years of the West Sussex Fire Brigade, 1948-1998* (The Oakwood Press, 1999)

McCann, Timothy J., 'From Frattenbury to Redminster: the Chichester Novels of Victor Whitechurch' in *Chichester History* 28, pp. 28–36 (The Journal of the Chichester Local History Society, 2012)

McCann, Timothy J., 'From Selchester to Wrenchester: the Chichester Detective Novels of J. S. Fletcher' in *Chichester History* 29, pp. 26–33 (The Journal of the Chichester Local History Society, 2013)

Revd W. R. W. Stephens, *Memorials of the Cathedral Church of Chichester* (London, 1876)

Hopkins, G. Thurston and Hopkins, R. Thurston, *Literary Originals of Sussex* (Alex J. Philip, Gravesend, 1936)

Thomas Gordon Willis, *Records of Chichester* (Chichester, 1928)

Printed Novels

Fletcher, Joseph Smith, *The Lost Mr Linthwaite* (1927)

Fletcher, Joseph Smith, *The Murder in the Pallant* (1927)

Fletcher, Joseph Smith, *The Paradise Mystery* (1920)

Whitechurch, Victor Lorenzo, *Concerning Himself: The Story of an Ordinary Man (1909)*

Whitechurch, Victor Lorenzo, *The Dean and Jecinora* (1926)

Whitechurch, Victor Lorenzo, *Mixed Relations* (1929)